DAŠA DRNDIĆ

CANZONE DI GUERRA

NEW BATTLE SONGS

Translated from the Croatian by
Celia Hawkesworth

D1439378

CONTENTS

LITTLE PIONEERS

Jadranka said: *Don't go.*

Father said: *You're right to go.*

Nenad said: *If only I could go.*

Jasna said to Sara: *Your mum's capable, you'll be fine.* Three years earlier (when we moved from Belgrade to Rijeka in Croatia), Jasna had said to Sara: *Your mum's hopeless, she's never achieved anything.*

Laura asked: *Will you write to me about how bad things are?* (When I wrote that things were all right, Laura stopped talking to me.)

My brother said: *I'm going to America, that's where I was born.* (He didn't go anywhere.)

Only my sister Lena sighed: *I'll miss you.* But she lived in Slovenia.

I had applied for a small managerial post. I didn't get it. The newspapers wished me a safe journey.

I read Dovlatov.

I read Krleža.

I read Brodsky.

Dovlatov was big and strong. He downed two litres of vodka a day. He spent seventeen years in Petrograd writing, but no one published any of it. He went to America, became well-known and after twelve years, in 1990, he died. He was forty-nine. Before that his daughter had asked him: *Are you happy now?* He replied: *No.*

After living in Rijeka for three years, Sara finally summoned the courage to ask for frankfurters using the Croatian and not the Serbian word.

Vesna told me that someone in a Croatian bank had said that she couldn't understand Serbian at all.

There's little Lulu from Somalia. Her father speaks French, English and German, as does her mother. Her mother is not from Somalia but of half-Polish, half-Hungarian origin and she was born in America. She asks Lulu from Somalia: *Qu'est-ce qu'il y a dans ta soupe?* Lulu says: *Il y a des carrotes, des pommes-de-terre, chicken and noodles and je veux un ice-cream maintenant.* She asks the waiter: *A glass of voda, please.* Lulu's not yet five. Everyone understands her.

It's a sunny winter's day. The sky is electric blue as it can only be in Paris or on the Adriatic when there's a north wind. Sara is saying goodbye to her girlfriends in the pizzeria under the building where we live. I walk and sing (to myself).

Rijeka is divided by a railway line. In Rijeka trains pass slowly through the city. Trains completely block out the view of the sea. This makes the city seem smaller.

There are several benches along the Quay. They're used by prostitutes and old people. The old people rest from standing, because the benches are opposite various administrative offices in which the old people spend a long time waiting in queues. The old people wear old clothes and worn-out shoes. Old people find it hard to get used to new clothes. The old men don't shave every day. The old man beside me takes a bun out of his shopping bag and sucks it. The way my granny Ana used to suck old toast because her teeth were no use anymore. There's a carrot poking out of his bag.

The sky is electric blue, says the old man.

The prostitute is no more than nineteen. She's got a small pale yellow towel poking out of her bag. The prostitute is eating salami. It's midday.

My mum sent me this, says the prostitute.

I'm sitting in the middle, between the old man and the prostitute, and I'm not eating anything.

The shape of your face isn't at all Serbian, my colleague R. V. in Belgrade had said. *You'll have to leave,* she also said.

In Rijeka everyone told me: *Tone down that Serbian accent.*

Dovlatov wrote about Spivakov.

As a Jew in the Soviet Union, Spivakov experienced a lot of unpleasantness. Even though he was called Spivakov and not Spivberg or Spivman. After all kinds of tribulations, the authorities permitted him to give a recital in the USA. When he arrived at the Carnegie Hall, he found a crowd from the American League for the Defence of Jews. They were holding up placards reading: **KGB agents – out!** They were shouting: **Fighting for the rights of Soviet Jews!**

When the concert began, Spivakov was bombarded with tins filled with red paint. Spivakov was completely red.

That was a long time ago. It's nothing like that now. Spivakov is internationally famous now. Among the most famous.

My little pocket mirror doesn't encompass all the lines on my face. It can only take in a small part of my chin. I'm grateful to my little pocket mirror.

The old man and the prostitute lean towards me, that is, towards my little mirror.

The old man says: *Just for a moment, my eye hurts.*

The prostitute says: *Let me just look at this tooth. It's loose.* She says that with a very wide-open mouth.

You've got hairs poking out of your nose, Sara told me at the bus station, where there were a lot of people. I pretended not to hear.

You've got dandruff, she added. *And that coat looks dreadful on you and you're fat.* The bus came so she stopped. In the bus, I told her: *I'm not buying you any more Kinder eggs.*

In the library they hadn't let me take the translation of *Catcher in the Rye* for Sara to read, because it was printed in the Cyrillic script. The librarian had whiskers and a lot of hair in her armpits.

The old man was chomping noisily on his dry bread.

The prostitute was chewing her dry sausage.

I took out some cherry sweets and offered them to the others. The three of us munched.

I said: *I'll take you for cakes.*

The old man said: *I've booked a place in the graveyard.*

The prostitute said: *There are a lot of suicides in Vojvodina.*

That didn't interest me as I was intending to go on living, in Canada. I didn't have anyone in the graveyard in Rijeka in any case.

At the cake-shop the waitress told us: *We don't sell baklava anymore.*

The old man said: *I like jam doughnuts best.*

The prostitute said: *I need a dentist.*

In the cake-shop we heard a direct broadcast of two acrimonious debates taking place in the Parliament. One about Istrian cattle, the other about Lipizzaner horses.

In the cake-shop, the old man said: *I'll come to see you off.*

I knew he wouldn't as he'd be asleep. Old people go to bed early, and we'd be leaving Rijeka at three in the morning.

The prostitute said: *I'll come too.*

That was also impractical as prostitutes generally work at night, when old people are sleeping. So, no one would be seeing us off.

Afterwards, when we arrived, I wrote to everyone. For the Christmas and New Year holidays. I sent 47 cards, nine to Belgrade, three to Israel, two to America, two to South Africa, one to Paris, one to Slovenia, one to Amsterdam, the rest to Croatia. Five people replied from Croatia, three from Belgrade and from the other countries – everyone, because they were nostalgic. That didn't surprise me. I'd lost ten kilograms for Canada. I looked quite good. Later, in Canada, I put them all back on. I took two evening outfits with me which I never wore. I took a white Toledo tablecloth for twelve people, which I never used. I took a large silver platter, which I later cleaned with Vim.

Fatima had left Croatia two days earlier. She had wanted to go to Australia, but she ended up in Novi Sad. She gave me a little badge, with *Fatima* written on it. Otherwise, in Croatia she told everyone to call her Seka (*Sis*). I attached the little badge to my coat. At the airport everyone thought I was called Fatima. In Croatia at that time, it wasn't a good idea to be called Fatima. It was better to be called Grozda, say. If that wasn't possible, then at least Vesna, Ivana, Maja or Ankica. Or perhaps Ada.

On the building of the Tuberculosis Clinic, someone had written **Turks go back to Bosnia!** That was where we had our lungs examined, because the Canadian authorities stipulated that only healthy, clean lungs should enter their country. My lungs are healthy, as are Sara's, needless to say. On the image of my lungs today you can't see that there was once a bit of a problem. The doctor said: *Give me your family history.*

I confessed everything:

Mother: open cavities, 1942. Later, cancer of the uterus, with metastases on the lungs. Died 1978. Sister, brother and I: distended hilum, early stage of process.

The doctor wrote everything in my notes and handed them to me. Then I took them to the office that sends them to Canada.

The following day, I went back to the office that sends the results of medical examinations to Canada. *I need those results for a competition in Croatia. I'll bring them back tomorrow.*

The assistant was very helpful. She was obviously a fighter against the drain of brains from the Homeland.

I threw away the notes the doctor had written. I went back to the Tuberculosis Clinic, with the words **Turks go back to Bosnia** written on it. This time with Sara, so that I wasn't recognised. I said: *I've lost the results of the examination.*

The assistant said: *You have to see the same doctor.*

Sara was horrified because I'd told her the whole story.

The doctor asked: *Has anyone in your family suffered from tuberculosis?*

I exclaimed: *Heaven forbid!*

The doctor also said: *Your heart is enlarged.*

That's from swimming, I said.

In her report for the Canadian authorities, the doctor wrote the nicest and best things about me. We were suitable for entry into that large, rich country. Especially Sara. She was so pure and healthy.

We were driven to Zagreb airport by a driver who offers funeral services. His car was the biggest and the only one where we could fit our four enormous suitcases, bought in Trieste for 73,000 lira each. The driver gave me an extremely significant letter to take to a distant relative of his who lives in Canada. He told me: *Be sure to find him. I want to go to Canada too.*

I asked him: *Do you have a reserved graveyard space?*

He said: *No. I'm from Bosnia.*

LITTLE UNFINISHED STORY

INTRODUCTION

There is a lot of literature about pigs. There is almost no genre of the written word into which pigs have not worked their way. They are found in science (veterinary, biological, medical), in literature (essays, poetry, belles-lettres), not to mention film and painting. As far as life is concerned, here too, in our everyday life, pigs are all around us, and their destiny in the development of civilisation and technology is increasingly bizarre. The bizarre destiny of pigs is our reality.

A BRIEF HISTORY OF THE ORIGIN OF VIETNAMESE POT-BELLIED PIGS

Most breeds of domestic pigs originated from the European wild pig, which in turn is thought to come from the Chinese breed *Sus vittatus* (or *Sus indicus*) and the Indian, *Sus cristatus*. Wild pigs are considered nocturnal omnivores. The pot-bellied pig is a direct descendant of the wild pig, that is the boar, from the genus

Artiodactyl, sub-genus *Suiformes*, family *Suidae,* breed *Sus,* type *Scrof.* Pot-bellied pigs have existed in Europe and Asia for 40,000 years now, in territories from the Pacific to the Atlantic and from the Mediterranean to Siberia. It is believed that they were kept as pets by some Chinese rulers eight thousand years ago.

There are numerous breeds of pig. Today's European and American pigs have come into being on the whole through cross-breeding, in other words man has intervened and, in addition to pigs of the usual size, produced also this miniature type. Of the large breeds some of the best known are the Yorkshire, White Chesters, American Landrace pigs (of Danish origin), Hampshire (USA), Berkshires (England), Polish-Chinese (USA), spotted, Herefords, Tamworths. The small pigs include: the miniature Homel pig, also known as the Sinclair and produced in the Homel Institute of the University of Minnesota, in 1949;the Pittman Moore pig (also from the USA); the Hanford miniature (which saw the light of day in the Hanford laboratory, USA, 1958); the Göttingen miniature (Germany, 1980); the Ohimi pig (Japan, 1945); the Lee Sung miniature (Taiwan, 1975); the Yukatan miniature (Mexico, 1960); the Yukatan micropig, and so on. It is interesting that the Vietnamese pot-bellied pig was not crossbred, and does not represent various breeds of a single genus, but is rather indigenous, and includes several types: Mong Cai (North East Vietnam); I (West Vietnam); Co (Central Vietnam); Heo Moi (South Vietnam). It is only recently, with the migration of small Vietnamese pot-bellied pigs to other continents, that they have been crossed with large local pigs. That's enough of that.

PIGS IN SOCIALIST YUGOSLAVIA

In the Balkans, the pig is a cult-animal, the more so the further east you go. I remember pre-holiday days, especially before New Year, because of the market stalls piled high with little clean pink suckling pigs. When there was no more room on the stalls, the peasants would arrange the piglets, dead, scalded, smooth, all dolled-up, in the open boots of their cars, even on their roofs, while snow creaked under the feet of passers-by, customers and observers. Pigs would also be seen hanging on fat metal hooks in the window of almost all the butchers in town, upside down, sometimes decorated with twinkling ribbons used for New Year decorations, with a couple of baubles to boot, to be properly festive. Before the larger state or popular festivals, our socialist towns, swamped with suckling pigs, big pigs, and little pigs, used to exhale a blessed, indisputable sense of community. Bakers were all booked days in advance, people swarmed through the streets, carrying huge black trays with their chief 'booty' to their homes, to their festively prepared tables.[1]

Further west, but still in the Balkans, the cult of roast suckling pig did not emit the authenticity so characteristic of their eastern neighbours. For instance, in the western Balkans (mainly in towns)

---

1 *PREPARING A PIG: In our country large pigs are usually slaughtered in winter … That's when they are fattest, because their fat and bacon are thickest. The task of slaughtering and preparing individual parts of the pig is not exactly a simple one, and a lot of care and practice is required for it to be done properly. The pig is first killed and then washed in hot water… then the bristles are removed with a sharp knife… The shorn pig is then hung up, usually on a tree or any other suitable place. Then the stomach is slit down the middle lengthways and the stomach and intestines removed while they are still warm. Then the spleen, kidneys and liver, along with the lungs and heart…* Dika Marjanović-Radica, instructor at the Domestic Science Institute, Dalmatian Cookery, 2nd, expanded edition, Journalism-Publishing Company Slobodna Dalmacija, Split, 1951.

in the pre-holiday, New Year fever, activities involving pigs and their culinary processing appeared artificial, like a forced but feeble imitation, like a kind of obsessive neurosis infecting the people as a whole. The way the 'nation' in the western Balkans practised godlessness, the way it had practised Yugoslavism and brotherhood, was the way it also roasted pigs. The way it now practises Catholicism and chokes on greasy noodles. And people wonder secretly whether sour cabbage is a Serbian dish; whether its preparation is perhaps an act of sacrilege to the homeland.

In the western Balkans (where an outer wall rears up for one to jump over), what is authentic, original, natural, 'national' – are turkeys. And poultry in general.[2] Feast days, especially winter ones,

---

2 *INSTRUCTIONS FOR POULTRY: Poultry may be slaughtered throughout the year, but every species has its season in terms of the taste and moistness of the meat. In winter old hens are best, because they are hard to digest in summer, young castrated cockerels (capons) are also best in winter. Chicks are best in late spring and through the summer from May and the whole of August. Tame fattened ducks are best from July and throughout the winter, until January, but October sees the start of the turkey season, which lasts until March. When poultry are slaughtered, they should be plucked while they are still warm, because the meat is then tastier than if the birds are scalded with hot water. Care must be taken not to pull off the skin … When the feathers have been plucked, the birds are scorched with burning paper and the hairs and pointed stubs in the flesh removed by hand. Then a cut is made at the base of the neck, through which the gullet, gizzard and windpipe are pulled out. At the lower end of the body, between the legs, another cut is made crosswise and the intestines and stomach removed. The intestines are carefully and slowly removed, along with the stomach and liver. On the lower bottom part of the body the intestinal opening is trimmed away… The pointed stubs are removed from each wing, the beak and lower jaw are cut off, the claws are removed and the poultry washed if possible in running water. If the birds are to be roasted, then the neck and two outer parts of the wing are also cut off… When poultry is selected at market, already killed and cleaned, one should ensure that the skin is pinkish or yellowish in colour. The type and taste of the meat depends mainly on the way the poultry have been fed. In our country it is customary to give turkeys a small glass of brandy the day before they are slaughtered to make the meat tastier and softer. Geese are given a little crushed coal to make their*

and turkey, not with baked sauerkraut but with sour cabbage, that is the glory of the Catholic west-Balkan culinary outer wall. Turkey with noodles (here they are again), turkey roasted with olives, charcoal-grilled turkey, and in more recent times – Istrian turkey in a hundred ways – with truffles, as cutlets, turkey stew, turkey cooked under embers, turkey 'à la Motovun'. Turkeys are clean, they're not fat (like pigs), when they're brought onto the table they look noble, as in American films. In the western Balkans, for a festive meal, a pig or a turkey may also be replaced by a roast ham. Absolutely. Not to mention smoked bacon. Just as in the eastern Balkans, for festive celebrations, roast pork may be replaced by roast turkey. And the circle closes. With ham and bacon, we return to pigs, in the western variant, with suckling pig and roast turkey we are in the eastern variant, and all that is connected by bacon, kidneys, sweetbreads and tripe – the edible parts of an ordinary pig.

After the war, in socialist Yugoslavia skyscrapers began to spring up rapidly, accompanied by songs of freedom and construction on the lips of eager builders, because socialist Yugoslavia had to become an industrial country and absolutely not, heaven forbid, remain (or become) an agricultural stock-raising paradise. Peasants scurried into the towns, dragging with them their hens, their sheep, their families and – their pigs. Since there were no adequate gardens, yards, pastures or cultivatable land around the skyscrapers, the mostly small apartments with mostly small bathrooms were

---

flesh moister and they are not fed for 18 hours before they are slaughtered. If possible, it is best to raise poultry at home. Females – hens, have finer and tastier meat, only castrated cockerels (capons) are known for their moist flesh… When live birds are purchased, one should establish that they are healthy, whether their eyes are bright, their beak closed and crest red, and that they are not old, which can be ascertained by their feet… Dika Marjanović-Radica, instructor at the Domestic Science Institute, Dalmatian Cookery, 2nd, expanded edition, Journalism-Publishing Company Slobodna Dalmacija, Split, 1951.

transformed into chicken coops and pigsties. The mild spring nights echoed with the nostalgic grunting of pigs and clucking of hens as a memento of past days of authentic village living. With subdued melancholy, the new citizens of the new towns, exchanging their fields and their forests, their external and internal spaces for asphalt, lived an imitation of tribal life; they practised their pathetically dislocated collectivity in surroundings of extreme individualism.

Brandy was brewed on electric cookers and pigs were slaughtered in reinforced concrete shelters. Knives were sharpened and blood coursed down the drains of built-in enamel baths. And song soared and a medley of folk dances wound round the narrow stairways, sometimes fifteen floors to the street. And in the street, all of this longing, singing, roaring, grunting, blood, sausages, offal, innards, merged with the din of the towns coming into being. The new socialist man was being born.

Today that Odyssey of the new socialist man is over. In great fury, sickened by himself and his own acceptance of the imposed alteration of his genealogical code, he reared up, he shouted, he destroyed towns, he forged himself a path to his mental pastures and now he is calm and ecstatic. He squats bewildered on the ashes of his past. Roast suckling pig and even roast turkey are things he only dreams of now.

A SCIENTIFIC DISCOVERY IN
CONNECTION WITH PIGS

Recently published research by the British endocrinologist Dr Vinod Patel confirms that confined pigs, forcibly moved away from their familiar surroundings, die abruptly. If the confinement of the pigs lasts after they have been moved, death is almost inevitable. That is probably why, after several years of endeavouring to adapt to their new surroundings, sows and boars disappeared from the towns of the Yugoslav community of nations and nationalities. Dr Patel's research also confirms that many condemned people die in custody before they reach their prison cell. It is believed that death, in pigs as in people, comes as a result of disturbances in the endocrine system of both species, which causes the undue secretion of a particular hormone. A contemporary illness has acquired a contemporary name: Porcine Stress Syndrome.

WHAT DO (SOME) IMMIGRANTS DO IN CANADA
AFTER THE COLLAPSE OF SOCIALIST YUGOSLAVIA?

Sara's song: In the shower, when she thinks I can't hear her, Sara sings: *What can we do to make things better, what can we do to make things better. La-la-la-la, grass so green, la-la oh heart of mine, la-la-la-la!* In the Istrian style.

Boris's story: *Yes, there was a war and we were, in a way, forced to leave, but in the end, in the end, it's our decision.*

Boris is talking to a journalist from Canadian state radio on an underground platform. In the background a violinist is playing a Hungarian czardasz, passers-by hurry, the scene is almost filmically all-encompassing and complete. Pizzicato.

There are so many excellent musicians in Canada. I don't think I'm good enough to play in the underground. Really. You don't have to do an audition, did you know that?

In his apartment, Boris takes out his violin and talks to a journalist from Canadian state television. As he talks, he plucks at the strings and talks about his violin worth fifteen thousand German marks that went up in flames in Sarajevo. Boris does not seem at all sad. He even often laughs.

I went into a shop selling musical instruments, just in case. There was a Chinese man at the counter. I asked him whether he hired out violins. He said, well no, but I'll give you one, you don't need to pay anything, he said. Keep it for three months; if you like it, you can pay, if you don't bring it back. He was the first person in Canada to offer me anything without asking a whole lot of questions. He didn't even ask for any identification. He just asked me whether I knew what was happening with Bosnian wood. Because Bosnian wood was very famous. I read somewhere that even Stradivarius made violins out of Bosnian wood. It was exported from Bosnia to Italy. Today I don't know whether there's any wood left in Bosnia.

Branko's story: *The first winter it was mostly old people who died. They couldn't keep warm. I watched old ladies, perfectly dressed, in fur coats, they wore fur coats, and I watched them collecting twigs in the parks, thin, damp twigs, in fact just the remains of what others had already cut up. And you could see that they'd once been ladies, real upper-class ladies. Eighty percent of the trees in Sarajevo parks were felled.*[3]

David's story: *We came to Canada in order to start a new life and we thought that, with time, we'd become part of the middle class. Ha! What an outmoded concept! Because the middle class is dying out. And that is very, very bad for contemporary society. We are returning to the old times in which a small ruling class held virtually everything in its own hands; today only technology has progressed, so that small ruling*

---

3 *Trees are very expensive, especially if they are used for heating or cooking. In Sarajevo the price reached 450 DM a metre. That's why it's necessary to use every alternative form of raw energy. We recommend the following:*

a) Plastic packaging from US lunch-packs. It reaches a very high temperature and is good for boiling water.

b) Cardboard boxes from the same lunch-packs. They contain quite a lot of resin and cut into strips create an excellent fire for cooking and heating.

c) Home-made briquettes are a special discovery. They are made from newspapers. The pages are soaked in water, crumpled and pressed hard into balls the size of a hand then left in the sun to dry. With a little patience you can make them yourself. Briquettes like this are an exceptional fuel for cooking soups, vegetables, pies, and if you have been industrious and have plenty of them, they are also excellent for heating rooms.

d) The plastic packaging of bottles also reaches a high temperature. Use it broken into small pieces and exclusively in closed stoves. It creates a lot of smoke and tar.

e) Less valuable wood. This is used for packaging for fruit and similar (fir). Its calorific value is minimal but it is useful for heating water and saving higher quality wood (hornbeam, beech).

f) Keep hornbeam, beech, oak, pine, ash, processed wood (chipboard, block-board) and other quality and calorific wood for dishes that require a high heat.
Enesa Šeremet: *How to survive on humanitarian aid*, WHO, UNHCR, WFP, Zagreb, 1994.

class controls you more easily, channels your behaviour, your way of life, more easily. Without a healthy middle class, society cannot advance.

(The Canadian radio reporter was astounded and offended. He couldn't understand what David was jabbering about. As he drank his coffee, the Canadian radio reporter was discreetly irritated that the story he was preparing didn't contain enough of the tragic and sensational, it lacked a certain *je ne sais quoi* that would get listeners' artistic juices flowing on a Sunday morning.)

Almira's interjection: *Some people thought they were coming to the promised land, while others quickly realised that there were no promised lands.*

David's story: *Over there, where you could barely make a living, you were still contented. There was always someone who would think for you. People were somehow modest. And somehow contented. There weren't many insatiable people, there weren't many who were terribly rich. There was no reason to work very hard. People understood: we're not rich, but we do have time.*

Branko's story: *Overnight you become a person without anything. A person without property, without money, without land. You have nothing. First there were some gunshots, then you could hear shelling in the distance. That sounded like fireworks. Exactly like fireworks. Then those 'fireworks' came ever closer. Just two weeks later the explosions had become pretty strong. That meant that the shells were right here, really close. A friend told me that he was in the street when he heard an explosion. Then he saw a dog, there were a lot of abandoned dogs in Sarajevo at that time, and the dog was running through the streets carrying a piece of human flesh in its teeth. Someone had been killed in that explosion, and that flesh was still living, that flesh in the dog's mouth was alive, it was pulsating.*

It was warm in the passageways of the underground. On borrowed guitars, trumpets, saxophones and electric organs musicians played, people for the most part from East-European countries, for the most part with university degrees, people who had passed auditions. In the busy, noisy streets overhead, the wind whipped you, your fingers froze.

Marko's story:

Marko: *Which would you like, spicy Italian or Polish?*

Passing man: *Polish.*

Marko: *Something to drink?*

Passing man: *Coca-Cola.*

Marko (to the Canadian radio reporter): *I never dreamed that I'd be selling hot-dogs and sausages in Toronto. I thought I'd make more of a success of my career. Because, excuse me… Hi! Spicy Italian or Polish?*

Passing woman: *Hot-dog.*

Marko: *First I taught literature at a secondary school, later I was a lecturer at the university. I also worked as an editor for a publisher and wrote literary criticism. Then, I'm a poet. Yes, I've had books published. Excuse me… Hi! Spicy Italian or Polish? Three dollars please… Three hot-dogs? Right away. Well-done or medium?*

Passing man: *Medium; wrapped.*

Marko: *I don't know. Canadian people's problems seem comic to me. In my country a lot of people died.*

Passing woman: *We're ungrateful. We don't know how lucky we are…*

Marko: *Well-done, you said?*

Passing woman: *Not too well-done, medium well-done…*

Marko: *On its way. Those problems… Hi! What would you like, spicy Italian or Polish? My mother was born in Croatia. I was… Hi! I'm a mixture. I'm a mixture of nationalities from former Yugoslavia. From Goražde. Have you heard of Goražde? No? Goražde is a town with one of the most tragic fates in this war. Massacres. My mother* spent two years and two months there during the war. Then she had to run away because she couldn't legally leave the town. And my aunt was killed… Excuse me. Hi! Spicy Italian or Polish?

Branko's story: *Dinner: spring onion with a few drops of vegetable oil and two slices of bread. That was an excellent dinner.[4] But the worst thing was that I hadn't even started to eat when two shells exploded in the neighbourhood and all the glass shattered, right beside me. Up until then I had believed that the war was happening somewhere else, far away. I didn't eat. My plate was full of tiny pieces of glass. Window glass. I was left hungry. That was the worst.*

Enes's story: *I'm from Sarajevo as well. I've been in Canada for a year and a half now, I've got refugee status. Otherwise, I'm an economist. I used to work in financial control and analysis. I don't like being on social support. I'm looking for work, it's hard. I attend a programme of classes for refugees. There we're taught how to look for work in Canada, how to create connections, how to write CVs, how to change profession. They teach us literature. In fact, it's a secondary school. They tell us: Join clubs run by your ethnic minorities. Then: Go to sports clubs and play sport. That's how contacts are made. Then: Find a hobby, there are a lot of hobby clubs.*

Marija's story: *When I went to that school, there were about thirty of us in the class, and it was well known that we all had some kind of*

---

4 *Suggestions for evening snacks:*
   CHICKEN PATE: 2 coffee cups of oil, 3 soup spoons of flour, 1 lunch-pack meal, no.6 or no. 11, 2 coffee spoons of powdered milk, 1 coffee spoon of salt.
   SOFT RICE CHEESE: 2 1/2 cups of rice, 2 litres of water, 1 1/2 soup spoons of vinegar, 1 1/2 soup spoons of powdered milk, 2 coffee spoons of salt
   UNUSUAL SPREAD: 4 soup spoons of flour, 1 soup spoon of powdered milk, 1/2 litre of water, 1 coffee spoon of salt, 2 coffee cups of oil, 'Vegeta' stock cube, pepper, mustard, parsley
   Enesa Šeremet: How to survive on humanitarian aid, *WHO, UNHCR, WFP, Zagreb, 1994.*

university degree. They gave us a maths test: addition and subtraction. The kind of problems set for my daughter in primary school. And before the class started, the teacher gave a little introductory speech about cleaning our teeth every morning and using deodorant and keeping ourselves clean and not smelling because in Canada a bad smell, a bad human smell is offensive to the public, whereas perhaps in our countries it wasn't.

Enes's story: *I think that many people make a mistake because they want to work in their own profession. I think that we have to change careers. We have to make a living doing jobs for which there is demand on the market. The ones needed in Canada. Canada needs electricians, bakers, plumbers, truck drivers. There is great competition for highly qualified jobs. My wife is a doctor, but in Canada it is very hard to get a permit to work in the medical profession. She needs five years. She has to take very difficult exams and she must have a year of working in Canada. My wife is now forty-four.*

David's story: *At home I worked in marketing and tourism. Otherwise, I'm a historian. When I arrived, I worked in a baker's, I sold bread and cakes. Then I worked as a secretary in a private office, for roughly six months, then I was dismissed. Then I went onto social security. In my case, my age is a handicap. I'll soon be fifty. Otherwise, I might have some hope. There are various conditions that incomers must fulfil. They have to have Canadian letters of recommendation and Canadian experience. What is so special about Canadian experience if a person already has twenty-five years' working experience? Book-keeping, for instance, is the same all over the world. Income-expenditure. It was invented by an Italian monk as early as the end of the fifteenth century. It's not rosy. The prognosis is gloomy.*

We sometimes wonder why we came, why did the Canadian authorities allow us to come in, why they import so many people? The conclusion sounds almost Marxist: they need cheap manpower. They need educated people to work for a minimal wage.

Boris's story: (Accompanied by constant plucking on the strings of the borrowed violin.) *A few days ago, I realised that I had become a little bored with Beethoven. The last work I played was the Mendelssohn violin concerto. Before that I had played Mozart and I worked for nine years as a music editor at Radio-Sarajevo. Here I work selling things. I sell violins, pianos, cellos in a music shop. I got my first job through some Sarajevo connections, on a building site. That was how I began my musical career in Canada. I swore that I wouldn't give up, whatever happened. Then they gave up on me. I was too slow. It's hard to build muscles in one's forty-eighth year.*

Later I worked with those poor creatures who go round companies with enormous sacks on their backs, offering all kinds of goods for sale. I had toys. Little remote-controlled cars, dolls that cry and wee. It was August and I knocked on the door of those companies asking: Might you be interested in Christmas presents for children? I worked from eight to eight. One day we were selling in the street, my supervisor and I, with those huge sacks on our backs, people passed, not looking, sympathising, we looked very small under those big sacks, it was hot, I didn't sell anything that day. Then I said I'm not going to carry those sacks anymore and that's that.

Every day I come across some new problem. So the problems pile up. The latest one is that I am increasingly shrinking the scope of my thoughts. It's not important whether you work as a deliveryman, a taxi driver or a builder, because with time that's what you become: a deliveryman, a taxi driver or a builder. How to put it, you have to simplify your thoughts. By simplifying your thoughts, you yourself become simpler, because you get used to simplifying your thoughts. In that process the brain also gets paler.

When we bought a car, it was a Jaguar, we didn't buy a Jaguar because of its speed, or because of its power. That car has style. When you sit in it, you feel… as a construction worker would say, like someone.

It's not only about the Jaguar, it's about a whole civilisation which I miss: footsteps on our rain-washed street in Sarajevo. The island of Pag in summer. Scents. The scent of pine needles and the bitter-tart scent of lemon blossom. Half of me is on Pag. I shall return to Pag to die in a hut somewhere and I'll keep goats. The scent of roses in Sarajevo gardens. That's what I dream about.

David's story: *People have to dream. Healthy people dream. They dream a lot.*

Almina's interjection: *We've got nothing to dream about. Here.*

David's story: *People dream even in prison.*

Almina's interjection: *They dream about freedom.*

David's story: *But I rarely dream. And when I do, they're wonderful dreams, always set in the same place, on a small island opposite Dubrovnik (I'm from Dubrovnik), Lokrum, I'm lying there in the sun, everything is quiet, calm, beautiful. In those dreams, I'm my own person, in my own place, no one bothers me. Oh, yes, I feel the rocks under my back, I breathe in the aroma of pine trees, maybe that's a dream about going back.*

Almina's interjection: *I'm going back.*

Branko's story: *It's nearly a year since I left Sarajevo. I came out in the winter of 1994. Through the tunnel.* The Canadian state radio reporter asks: *Is there a lift in that tunnel?* Branko says: *No. It's a hole. An ordinary hole. It's like going through hell. It's narrow, it's low, in some places not even a metre and a half. It was raining and the ground inside was made of clay and clay is slippery. I was wearing old shoes, completely worn out. They were very slippery as well. I kept falling into the mud. I was afraid of breaking my leg. There was no time for panic. All I could think about was getting out alive. I was carrying two bags. That was my whole property. Some photographs and a few documents. Certificates. I set off at four o'clock in the afternoon and the next day, around eight in the evening, I left Bosnia.*

Vesna's story: *We know that Canada can't offer us everything we had before. But a little dignity, at least. We are people too. I have to work for my children. All right, I want to work, but where? My husband wants to work as well, but where? There are some jobs we can't do because we have to improve our English, others because we have to improve something else, there's always something that needs to be improved. It's never enough. I'm an economist by training. I used to work as a social worker and allocated social security payments. Now I'm receiving social security. I know that I won't be able to use my training in Canada. I'm forty-two, I've got young children and I don't have the energy. The future? The future depends on how long I'll have the strength for physical work. I work like an animal. Eight hours a day in big houses. Those are houses on two floors, with one or two staircases, with four bedrooms, with rooms for resting, rooms for recreation, rooms for sunning oneself. There's not much sun here. The first thing the owner of one of the houses asked me was did I have Canadian experience. I asked her what I needed Canadian experience in, cleaning or living?*

Branko's story: *I'm convinced I'll find a job. I'm an electrician, I work in electronics, microprocessors, computers. I'll find work. When I arrived, I may have been a bit depressed, but I'm not anymore. How could I be depressed when Canada has offered us refugees somewhere to live and material support for a year, for accommodation and clothes. That's a big thing when you've got nothing. I'm grateful. I'm sure I'll find a job.*

Almina's interjection: *I'm not at all grateful. It's eyewash. They give us charity, but there's no work.*[5]

---

5 Outside the church quite a hundred men were waiting, dirty types who had gathered from far and wide at the news of a free tea, like kites round a dead buffalo. Presently the doors opened and a clergyman and some girls shepherded us into a gallery at the top of the church. It was an evangelical church, gaunt and wilfully ugly, with texts about blood and fire blazoned on the walls, and a hymn-book containing twelve hundred and fifty-one hymns […] There was to be a service after the tea, and the regular congregation were sitting in the well of the church below.

Vesna's story: *When I'm angry, I am very clear-headed. But that's not good for the family. The children feel the tension. Everyone's always rushing, rushing. There's no peace. It's all like a bad dream. It would never have occurred to me that something like this could ever happen. Never. This is an exodus. From one country to another, and the differences aren't great. Here we sleep peacefully, there's no shelling, but we're waging a different war. A war in the soul, a war in the head. Why did we come? We thought Canada was a country of great possibilities. I don't know why no one told us the truth.*

Sara's song: Sara keeps singing. Even two years later, she sings: *What can we do to make things better, what can we do to make things better. La-la-la-la, grass so green, la-la oh heart of mine, la-la-la-la!* In the Istrian style. And it has begun to irritate me because I don't know how to answer her and she keeps asking and looking at me.

Milan opened a little café. Sometimes Boris, Branko, David, Alma and Vesna met there. And others came. They'd all been in Canada

---

We ranged ourselves in the gallery pews and were given our tea; it was a one-pound jam-jar of tea each, with six slices of bread and margarine. As soon as tea was over, a dozen tramps who had stationed themselves near the door bolted to avoid the service; the rest stayed, less from gratitude than lacking the cheek to go. The organ let out a few preliminary hoots and the service began. And instantly, as though at a signal, the tramps began to misbehave in the most outrageous way. One would not have thought such scenes possible in a church. All round the gallery men lolled in their pews, laughed, chattered, leaned over and flicked pellets of bread among the congregation […] It was a queer, rather disgusting scene. Below were the handful of simple, well-meaning people, trying hard to worship; and above were the hundred men whom they had fed, deliberately making worship impossible. A ring of dirty, hairy faces grinned down from the gallery, openly jeering. What could a few women and old men do against a hundred hostile tramps? It was our revenge upon them for having humiliated us by feeding us. The scene had interested me. It was so different from the ordinary demeanour of tramps – from the abject worm-like gratitude with which they normally accept charity. […] A man receiving charity practically always hates his benefactor …

George Orwell: *Down and Out in Paris and London*, Penguin Books, London, 1982.

between one and four years. Boris had bought his Jaguar because the Croatian Credit Alliance lent him the money, but that meant that he had nothing left to pay for his Canadian citizenship. Boris was given some old cassettes of classical music that were now gathering dust because he didn't have time to listen to them. After four years of being in Canada, Boris hadn't been anywhere on holiday, he bought a bread-making machine (a lot of people from former Yugoslavia bought bread-making machines), his clothes seemed to have tightened on him. Boris looked increasingly like a salesman, one from back home. There was nothing recognisably Canadian about him.

Branko made it. He got paid work in his profession and opened a special savings account for his son's education. His son is five. He had his teeth fixed. He bought a dog, called Haris. His children talk to him more and more often in English.

David registered at university for a third time. He'll soon become a licensed accountant and at the end of the year he'll be calculating Canadians' tax. For that he doesn't even need an office. In commercial centres and markets you can hire a small space, 2×2 metres, enclosed by high blockboard. He's forgotten German. He's forgotten history. He's forgotten tourism. The only thing he hasn't given up is his long-term passion – expensive shoes.

Darko decorates other people's apartments. Darko is a qualified fine artist.

Saša works for a marketing company filling envelopes with advertisements for various goods and makes progress in that work with every day.

Hrvoje was dismissed from psychiatry when they convinced him that he didn't in fact need to be an intern. He bought a second-hand car and delivers pizzas.

Boško hangs off thick cords, cleaning skyscraper windows. Afterwards he takes analgesics.

Marko left, because he couldn't complete his doctorate while selling sausages. Now he's an editor in Budapest.

I write, because it's warm in the apartment and it isn't outside and because I don't have a coat and I don't have winter shoes, only those formal patent leather ones I bought in Trieste six years ago.

The Canadian radio presenter isn't, of course, particularly interested in all this. He's doing his job. His job is to introduce to the listeners a new category of fellow-citizens. The listeners have some difficulties with this, however, because it's not easy to recognise this new category of fellow-citizens in everyday life, because this new category of fellow-citizens is not yellow or black or slant-eyed, or bearded, nor do they wear saris, nor turbans, they aren't lame, they don't smell of curry, nor do they buy rice by the sack-full: These new, recently arrived fellow-citizens look just like them, so long-term residents can't go around smiling at them every five minutes, they can't offer them moral support which includes the Christian message: Welcome!

In these notes I haven't mentioned Goran (MA in Philosophy and former minister in the Government of one of the former Yugoslav republics, removed from his post by a nationalist governing body because of his non-nationalist views), who now just cooks for his large family. Goran (50) makes excellent cheese pies and speaks English fluently. I didn't mention a poet from Sarajevo who works in the storehouse of a famous fashion house unloading suits the price of which can reach twenty thousand dollars. I had no idea. That suits costing twenty thousand dollars exist. There's also a sculptor here, who works in a factory making decorative plaster casts for the ceilings of the houses of the rich. Asja's thyroid gland burst, her neck swelled right up, they say it was war stress. Then she shaved all her hair off, so now she looks like a typhus patient. That thing with the thyroid gland happened when she had found a job in a bookshop, at the counter. Now she translates famous Sarajevan writers into English, and no one wants to publish them because a lot of publishers prefer light literature. (Asja is, otherwise, a university lecturer, teaching English.) I didn't mention the handsome green-eyed pilot Faruk, who pushes wheelchairs around in a hospital geriatric department. I didn't mention Sanja the architect who looks after a handicapped child. There's a whole little colony of sad people who celebrate the First of May. Then they sing all kinds of songs from the distant nineteen-sixties and laugh. And they talk about the fact that this reminds them of the worst nights of war in Sarajevo, because they sang like that while they were being shot at from the hills of Pale.

On an underground platform I met a black woman who described her miniatures in detail. She collected them. She collected little violins, little guitars, little newspapers, little books, little people, little teapots, little trumpets, little houses, little railways, little furniture, little pieces of crockery, little pianos. If necessary, she ordered her little things (and people) from Europe, or she went to America to get them when she couldn't find what she wanted in Canada. She's making a whole new other world without herself knowing why. That new world she's making is full of tiny, barely visible details, just like the real big ones. Then I imagined how nice it would be to get us all together and shrink us then put us on that woman's shelf. But since many people had already imagined such things, I abandoned further contemplation on that theme.

WHAT DO (SOME OTHER) IMMIGRANTS DO IN CANADA AFTER THE BREAK-UP OF SOCIALIST YUGOSLAVIA?

1. When they arrive, they ask friends to look after the local money they have from the apartments they sold and they register for social security. (Because social security offices have the right to examine bank accounts and so on.)
2. Every Friday they get together in an Irish pub that has a terrace on its roof with a lot of plants, and they drink Irish beer.
3. When they have something to celebrate, they invite a lot of people and then they feed them well. They serve all manner of things from former Yugoslavia. When it's a matter of food, there's no prejudice, the national question doesn't arise.
4. The women wear a lot of pure silk blouses in pastel shades and little suits and slender-heeled shoes, leather of course.
5. In winter they go skiing, in summer to the Canadian lakes. Canada has a lot of perfectly managed Canadian lakes.
6. They go home to visit at least once a year and say how great it is here.
7. They say that they have come (the men that is, of course) to avoid being mobilised, but on the whole they are over forty. (The twenty-year-olds who haven't come have on the whole been killed.)
8. They say that all sides in this war are equally to blame, and when they are told that yes, they are to blame but absolutely not equally, they stop speaking to you.
9. They go to hear bands from their homeland when they play in Toronto because that's a connection with home.
10. Among themselves they speak Serbian, but when they're with you they say they speak Serbo-Croatian so as not to offend you.

When you say that you speak Croatian or Bosnian, they say those languages don't exist.

11. They are thrilled with Peter Handke.

12. Those who didn't come sent their children to Canada to study.

13. When they get Canadian citizenship, they intend to go back and carry on where they left off.

14. They are offended if a Bosnian or a Croat tells them that he has left Serbia. They ask, why on earth would they do that?

15. They are offended if a Bosnian or Croat doesn't read Slobodan Selenić, doesn't like Dobrica Ćosić and doesn't watch the film 'Pretty Village, Pretty Flame'.

16. They keep wanting to do the traditional Orthodox three-kiss greeting, and when you don't want to, they say 'I don't give a f...'.

17. They appropriate Sarajevo and the Adriatic Sea. They say, we're at home there, that's all our country.

18. They're glad that Mira Marković has been well received in Ljubljana, although, to be fair, they do always stress that she is ghastly, ghastly.

19. If you speak the ijekavian dialect they ask you where you're from so they know how to place you.

20. If one of them is putting on a play, and is a former colleague of yours, his wife phones to tell you the number you should call to book tickets.

21. When you say you're going home, they ask: 'To Belgrade?'

22. For them, it's as though this war hasn't happened.
And,

23. There are exceptions.

EXCEPTIONS

a) These exceptions are very different.

b) They've distanced themselves from those exceptions because they don't fit in.

c) Such an exception, for instance, is my former colleague, a sound-engineer, who sells televisions, torches and lightbulbs in a department store.

d) Such an exception is also thirty-year-old Dragan who has been trying for five years now to continue his postgraduate studies, but he can't because he sends everything he earns to his family so that they can buy a boiler or wood for the winter.

e) These exceptions aren't a pressure group.

f) The women among these exceptions travel for an hour or two to work, they get back at eight and then they cook. They don't even baulk at night shifts.

g) The local ethnic newspapers don't print interviews with these exceptions.

h) David is such an exception even though (some) Croats drove him out of Dubrovnik.

i) When they earn a bit of money, these exceptions celebrate in a small, ordinary Chinese or Lebanese restaurant.

j) These exceptions have friends from Sarajevo and other places.

k) These exceptions, like Marko, sell sausages in the street and then nearly go mad.

l) They are very lovely exceptions.

VIETNAMESE (POTBELLIED) AND
MINIATURE PIGS IN AMERICA

In 1985 the Canadian Keith Connell, otherwise employed at a zoo, imported eighteen potbellied pigs, four boars and fourteen sows, into the United States directly from Vietnam. Compared to the established prejudice about the appearance of pigs, these Vietnamese pigs look exotic – with strikingly black hair, saddle-shaped backs and a straight tail. They have a wrinkled face and a large, pendulous belly. According to various estimates, from the original core, in about ten years, the population of these pigs in the USA has now reached between two hundred and five hundred thousand, with the trend now decelerating.

Soon after their arrival on the American continent, pigs from Connell's herd were sold at various auctions of exotic animals, where they were advertised as a new kind of family pet. Breeders and promoters of Vietnamese potbellied pigs swamped the media with stories of the unusual pets, and the wave spread. The pigs were a hit.

Breeders pay up to thirty thousand US dollars for a pair of breeding Vietnamese pigs. Their offspring can barely satisfy demand. New potential buyers put themselves on waiting lists and may have to wait up to a year and a half. In order to increase the litters, some breeders cross Vietnamese pigs with indigenous breeds, producing 'mongrels' which they then palm off on buyers as 'pure-bred', 'original' potbellied porkers.

The market was flooded with new profiteers. Thanks to the pigs, breeders bought houses and cars and went on excursions. One woman, for example, bought a sow for four thousand dollars and with her first litter earned six times that. As far as is known, the highest price paid to date for a pig is thirty-seven thousand dollars.

Then the moods of the market did their thing. The pigs had done their job, it was no longer possible to earn much on them, and they became uninteresting as pets largely because it turned out that they weren't exactly adaptable. Abandoned small and not so small Vietnamese potbellied pigs roamed through the streets of towns. They came into parks, they reached the suburbs, rubbish tips and – the butchers.

As usually happens, one day the media published the tragic story of little Rufus, and in connection with him an initiative founded on absolute goodwill and general humaneness: REFUGE OPENS FOR ABANDONED AND REJECTED VIETNAMESE PIGS. THE REBIRTH OF LITTLE RUFUS.

Rufus had been the pet of seven male students who after a while concluded that he was in fact more of a burden to them than a source of amusement. He was too loud, too demanding, sometimes even aggressive. They shut him up in a cellar and invited the founders of the first refuge for abandoned pigs, who had been glorified in the media – Jim Brown and David Ronson – to come and get him.

Interest grew in the abandoned pigs. Organised groups of visitors from Japan, Australia, Germany, Britain and Belgium came to see how the Refuge functioned and whether they might found something similar in their own countries. New refuges sprang up all over the United States. Many of the pigs in them were only in transit, because a network was arranged to place abandoned and abused pigs in adoptive families.

In the families, however, the Vietnamese (potbellied) and miniature pigs had problems in adapting. There were changes in their behaviour, mostly as a result of being isolated from other pigs. The most prominent symptoms of such unacceptable behaviour in the pigs were: depression and withdrawal into themselves, insecurity, anger, fear and – aggression.

Those with experience in treating trauma in pet pigs say that they come across pigs that are not even aware of the fact that they are pigs; they are antisocial and have trouble accepting the collective (that is the other abandoned pigs which have already made friends – they don't know how to communicate with them, because their piggy language, as an integral part of their piggy identity, has been disrupted, even destroyed). In summary, their socialisation is a slow and difficult process.

Pigs are territorial animals and within their group establish a quite specific hierarchical order, in which every pig knows its place.

With house pigs such an order is upset, because the household threatens it. If the people there cross into his, the pig's territory (especially the place where he sleeps), the house pig can start to bite them, even to bark.

It's advisable to castrate house pigs, because they reach sexual maturity early and this can create problems. Given that the number of homeless pigs is growing, activists for the protection of unwanted, neglected and ill-treated pigs in America organise lectures and print brochures with instructions about how to ensure the pigs a peaceful and contented life in their new surroundings. With that they stress that the importation of these animals must finally stop because they can't easily adapt to surroundings that are not at all appropriate to their nature.

On the basis of personal experience, they, those volunteer activists of non-governmental and not-for-profit organisations, have found what makes a pig happy:

1. Fresh grass, especially clover
2. Rooting, especially after rain
3. Treats such as apples, melon, watermelon and fresh vegetables
4. Sunbathing

5. Being scratched on the stomach and flanks
6. Scratching themselves on trees, rocks, fences or each other
7. Associating with other pigs
8. Being wrapped in blankets or burying themselves in straw or hay when it's cold
9. Rolling in puddles or pools when it's hot
10. Exploring neighbouring woods

The enthusiasts Brown and Ronson succeeded in providing all of the above for their protegés, and more. On their farm in West Virginia, they offer unwanted, rejected, ill-treated Vietnamese pigs both professional veterinary care and conditions for healthy social-isation. *We treat each animal as an individual, as a unique entity, for no two pigs are the same, say Brown and Ronson for the press. Some adapt more easily and quickly to their new surroundings, others need more time. We don't hurry them. We want our pigs to realise that they are wanted, that they are living in a safe place, where they will not lack for human or animal warmth.*

Brown and Ronson also visit universities in America where they give lectures to students of veterinary medicine and their teach-ers about the behaviour of pigs and the psychological problems encountered by pigs brought up as house pets.

The community of porcine guardians is growing. United round the same goal, members of this community print newspapers, correspond, exchange experience, advise one another, organise porcine events, all for the wellbeing of imported and then neglected Vietnamese potbellied pigs.[6]

---

6 So Sandra Parson, in the pig lovers' weekly *Ziggy*, no. 5, 1996, writes, among other things: 'P.J. is an extremely intelligent and very charming pig. When we took him in, we weren't aware of how much care he would need. Both my husband and I work, so that P.J. was alone in the house all day. So, with heavy hearts, we decided to place him in a sanctuary, from where, we hoped he would be adopted. In the refuge P.J. was reborn. We visit him almost every weekend

In this whole story, however, the most striking is the warning directed through all available media by the Americans Brown and Ronson to their fellow-citizens and beyond: The import of house pets is a destructive act. Imported animals are forced to live in what is for them an unnatural environment, which often costs them both their physical and their mental health.[7]

---

and the changes are striking. There he got to know Lucinda, well-known for the acrobatic skills she performs with exceptional ease, as well as Star, who goes on his own to the nearby shop for yoghurt. P.J. and Star will take part in this year's Christmas parade, for which they have been preparing hard for weeks.' There are also heartrending letters composed by the pigs themselves. In the monthly *Lucky*, of 23 October 1996, a certain Bacon says, among other things: 'I was exposed to terrible violence, I was neglected and virtually confined. For three months, my owners kept me in the utility room and fed me exclusively on potatoes. They neither cleaned nor emptied my toilet. If I made a mess on the floor, they would hit me with a broom. They never took me out into the air, I never played with other little pigs. I even got an infection of the urinary tract because, when they ran out of potatoes, they gave me cat food. Now I've been saved. I am in absolute piggy heaven. I never dreamed that life could be so good. I have my own little house and a fence for scratching on. I've got lots of friends. I go out whenever I want, no one forbids me anything. Sometimes I even go fishing with my owners.'

7 The information about Vietnamese potbellied pigs quoted here is easily accessible: in libraries, on the Internet, in kiosks. The information quoted about pigs in the Balkans is on the whole known to us from the Balkans and probably to inhabitants of the former Eastern Bloc. Details about the emigrés from former Yugoslavia are irrelevant to people in the West. People like to look at events in the round, they like to have a complete picture, in order to understand certain events better. For instance, a column of 160,000 Ruandan refugees are trying to return to their homeland from Zaire. In Vase Miškina Street in Sarajevo an explosion eliminated a dozen people as they queued for bread. In the Sarajevo market a shell killed or injured eighty. All people without names. But here they remember little Rufus, P. J., Bacon and O. J. Simpson. People in the West put together details, little scenes from everyday life out of their own events, which are, thank goodness, abundant.

GLASSHOUSES AND SHITBALLS

I

My granddad wrote a letter to Tito.

Comrade President,

Forgive me for taking the liberty of writing you this letter. But I do so because I believe that it is necessary and useful that you too should be acquainted with its contents.

On 15.xi.1953, at the pre-election rally in Poreč, Comrade Karlo Mrazović took the floor, and at that same rally, as an advertised speaker, my son, Boris Radan was also expected, yes, as the candidate represent-ative of a group of citizens who had known him since 1941, as one of the first Partisan fighters, to make his pre-election speech.

By writing to Tito, he thought that he could rectify some injustices, political injustices, that had been done to his son, my father, and to him, himself. My grandfather had two sons. Political injustices had also been done to his other son but they were rather less significant than those that had befallen his first son, my father, because his second son was wiser and quieter and immediately after the war, he got a job with the UDBA secret services, while the first one was a journalist and in 1945 that was a significant difference.

However, as soon as my son Boris got up to speak, there was a hellish din from part of the organised audience who hurled a torrent of cries against my son: "Down with the fascist! Down with the bandit! Down with the imposter! Down with the traitor! Don't let the traitor speak!" And the like, so that for a long time the hellish yelling and whistling drowned out my son's every word.

I doubt that nowadays anyone in their right mind would write letters to the President. The President now is not Tito, and the times are rather different, although among today's political injustices and idiocies, there are astonishing similarities with those from the time of so-called communist Yugoslavia.[8]

You can imagine, comrade President, how I felt when I saw with my own eyes and heard the electoral terror being perpetrated against my son and the way the frenzied mob was insulting him, egged on and led by various Party functionaries in Poreč; how I felt when I saw for myself what kinds of lies and slanders were being sown among the ignorant people of our region, against my son and myself; and the way, to that end, the afore-mentioned functionaries abused not only the daily press, but also Rijeka Radio, through which my son Boris was invited to put himself forward as a candidate for the position of president of the local Italian party, Pelle.

---

8 A month after writing this text, I read in *Arkzin*: *Did you know that people write to the President? Did you know that despite all his duties as a statesman, supreme commander, husband, father, son-in-law, grandfather, historian, and historical figure, tennis-player and player of 'preference' ... the President manages also to read letters from the people?* In other words, even today people write to the President; in other words, some things repeat themselves.

My grandmother wrote Tito a letter as well. That grandmother was not the wife of the grandfather who wrote to Tito, and her letter (written with an old 'Pelikan' pen, and not tidily typed like my grandfather's, and full of grammatical mistakes, because my grandmother Ana had attended Italian schools and the letter 'h' did not feature in any of her pronouncements, so instead of 'home' she said 'kome', instead of 'hot' she said 'kot', instead of 'hotel', 'kotel' and instead of 'thank you' 'tank you'), her letters to the Marshal travelled packed in ugly blue envelopes.

I'm not defending the honour of my son or my family, but the truth, and, through the truth, democracy and freedom. I feel that it is my civic duty on the occasion of this unheard-of terror and scandal to mention the following:

This grandmother was not my father's mother, but my mother's. I know a lot about her, whereas I know little about my Istrian grandfather, roughly as much as fitted into his letters:

1. *With my two sons, Boris and Nikša, and my sick wife, I fled from Istria into the old Yugoslavia in the face of the Fascist terror, back in 1921.*
2. *I brought my two sons up, from an early age, in a freedom-loving, democratic and progressive spirit, so that in the old Yugoslavia both of them were in the Communist Youth Movement.*
3. *During their time at University in Belgrade, both my sons were persecuted and beaten up by the police, as communists.[9]*
4. *Both went to fight as early as 1941 and both were awarded the Partisans' Commemorative Medal.*

---

9 My father was beaten up by the chief of the Belgrade police, Kosmajac, in person.

5. *Both were members of the Local Committee of the Communist Party of Croatia for Istria and from the very beginning (1941) they managed the resistance movement in Istria, and I joined them in the forest in 1943, when I was released from fascist prison.*

6. *After the liberation, my son Nikša became a… , and my son Boris a…* (irrelevant).

7. *Finally, immediately after the liberation, in 1945, I was president of the Regional National Committee for Istria (in which position I had the honour to meet you, Comrade President, on the occasion of a reception of Polish leaders in Opatija in 1946), and I remained in that office until my retirement in July 1947. At which time I was decorated with the Medal II Class for services to the people.*

My grandmother from Split was a converted atheist, because during her youth, from the beginning to the middle of the century, it was more convenient to live in Split as a believer. My loud grandmother Ana changed her mind after the war: she stopped being a believer and stopped going to church, although she never became a communist. My grandfather Vjekoslav was no longer there then because he died as soon as they moved from Split to Zagreb, when my mother, then a medical student, starving, with open cavities on her lungs (the appearance of which I always connected with her activity as a member of the Communist Youth), when my mother was put in prison by the Ustashas, the Croatian fascists. She was twenty years old.

Zagreb, 23 April 1943.
I didn't see Lala again… Only Britva and Joža remained. One day, instead of Joža, I was met by Britva. He told me that there had been a security lapse at the Moslovac canal. There had been shooting, a courier was captured and some of those who were going to join the Partisans were killed…

44

Around four o'clock in the morning, 18th May 1943, the doorbell rang and several Ustasha agents, kicking the door, burst into the apartment. I succeeded in shoving my documents into my pyjamas while my mother and two brothers let them in. The Ustasha agents swarmed through the rooms and one of them approached me demanding that I immediately hand over the register of 'Partisan bandits'.

I understood that there had been a security lapse. The agent who searched my room did not make much effort; he looked tired probably from similar searches that night. They let me go to the bathroom. There I shoved the pages with agents' profiles into the toilet bowl…

They took me to my first interrogation. I waited until eight in the morning in an empty office. Only then did the investigator Kamber arrive. With some short breaks, he interrogated me for a whole day and a whole night, with threats, blows and abuse. They offered me chocolate and immediately afterwards beat me up… Then they took me to another room where there were a lot of weapons and bombs, and quite a few Partisan uniforms. They told me that Joža had confessed everything and it would be best for me to do the same. Then they brought Joža in barefoot behind me. He was completely disfigured. I said I didn't know him. Then they brought the courier for Maslavina in as well. I said I didn't know him either.

Joža, quite beside himself, was no longer the Joža from the Spanish war. He looked like a robot as he said: 'Come on, girl, why not talk, they'll shoot the three of us in any case.' They went on beating me and for quite a while I was unconscious… Ustasha agents kept coming in, swearing and threatening me. They wanted me to sign a document saying that I would be 'a loyal citizen of the Independent State of Croatia and that I would work for them'… I was saved by an Ustasha agent who worked for us…

As early as the nineteen-twenties, my grandfather Vjekoslav had begun talking about social and political injustices, particularly when he came back from Vienna, where he had spent time with communists.

In fact, it was like this:

I grew up knowing one grandmother and one grandfather; my mother's mother and my father's father. Both have died of course, as has my mother. My mother died fairly young, probably because of those open cavities on her lungs acquired as a Communist Youth, they had been treated, but that's where the cancer appeared that did for her. But perhaps the beatings she received in that Zagreb Ustasha prison also contributed to her death, as perhaps did the fact that she contracted an inflammation of her ear when she went running for medical help in 1948 because I was ill. No one will ever know.

There are two branches of my family: the one from the city of Split, on my mother's side, and the Istrian one, on my father's. They are both Croatian, so that when this new war broke out, in 1990, when socialist Yugoslavia fell apart and when blood cells began to be counted, I didn't have a problem. Some may even have come to love me because of the purity of my Croatian blood. The purity of my Croatian blood soothed some people and protected me in seeking employment.

On the other hand, the fact that I had been absent for many years from the then Socialist Republic of Croatia, my godlessness, then some words of Turkish and generally Oriental origin, with a particular flavour, which would crop up in my speech and writing, could disturb people in power and those who would have been in a position to help me.

I was fourteen when I discovered Schiller and Goethe in the Gothic script in my grandmother Ana's small, uncomfortable Zagreb apartment, books my Split grandfather, by then already deceased, used to read. I also found a Hamsun in a leather binding on which was printed HUNGER in gold lettering. People are now writing about Hamsun again, in one way or another, just as they write about

Mile Budak[10] in one way or another. I read the Hamsun immediately and I remembered it well, although that was not expected of me at fourteen years old. Today, when some people write about Hamsun, they mention those shoes of his and Dubrovnik, as though his shoes were important. (I know nothing about the details of Mile Budak's intimate life, although I believe that people will be writing about them as well in the foreseeable future. I do know, however, that when Artuković[11] and Pavelić fled from Croatia, Budak fled as well, while Hamsun did not leave his native Norway. I know that, as a writer, compared to Hamsun, Budak is insignificant, (not to mention in comparison to Ezra Pound).

I don't have copies of the letters which my Split, and later Zagreb grandmother, wrote to Tito. I'm not even sure what those letters, sent to the Marshal's residence in Belgrade, were about. A hazy recollection surfaces, something connected with the paintings of a certain Paško Vučetić, painter and sculptor, otherwise my grandmother Ana's uncle, otherwise a Croat, otherwise married to a certain Marija, a Serb.

Paško Vučetić's paintings are displayed in the National Museum in Belgrade, some of his sculptures of boys from the Čukur fountain still ornament Belgrade streets today, and there is one in the cemetery where Marija and Paško are buried, along with my mother,

---

10 Mile Budak (30 August 1889 – 7 June 1945) was a Croatian politician and writer best known as one of the chief ideologists of the Croatian fascist Ustasha movement, which ruled the Independent State of Croatia during World War II in Yugoslavia from 1941–45 and waged a genocidal campaign of extermination against its Roma and Jewish population, and of extermination, expulsion and religious conversion against its Serb population. {Translator's note, *Wikipedia*}

11 Andrija Artuković was a Croatian lawyer, politician, and senior member of the ultranationalist and fascist Ustasha movement, who served as the Minister of Internal Affairs and Minister of Justice in the government of the Independent State of Croatia during World War II. {Translator's note, *Wikipedia*}

because my mother died in Belgrade as that's where we were living at the time. Paško and Marija are lying in large coffins made of walnut wood. I saw that when the tomb was opened, and they placed my mother beside them in a small, cheap black urn made of tin, which was unpleasant to look at: my mother, so abruptly reduced, so crushed (had her gold fillings remained, do teeth burn, do teeth burn?), being lowered into the big concrete tomb where it was very cold. I think that my grandmother Ana had actually wanted to have Paško's remaining works transferred to Split and that was why she wrote those letters to Tito.

I never heard my grandmother Ana speak passionately about Croatian-ness, but today, when I remember Paško and her letters, I believe that in those apparently comical and in the end pointless efforts to get Paško, albeit dead, through his paintings, back to where he was born, there was a suppressed, hidden, instinctive need to define her own sense of belonging. It is only now, decades later, that I have found a little schoolbook of my mother's (she's not here, so I don't know any details), a little blue canvas notebook, from elementary school in Split. It was dated 1937, when my mother was fourteen, with plaits round her head and a perfectly sewn dress of flowery cotton. Those perfectly sewn dresses on all the photographs she left me were unique fashion items, rare in the wardrobes of tradesmen's families in Split in the nineteen-thirties. It can't be seen on the photographs, but my grandmother Ana told me, because she was a seamstress and had fourteen employees she was very proud of and she sewed for the ladies of Split whose children had pianos in their parlours, where my mother would go and practise, because she had a hundred percent perfect pitch and had she not become a psychiatrist, she would have become more famous than our Zinka Kunc. The unique models worn by my mother, were created by my grandmother Ana from remnants of the materials brought by the ladies of the Split

Jet Set for their suits, blouses, dresses and skirts made of silk, geor-gette, wool or tulle. That is why, in all the photographs from her youth, my mother is elegant and smiling but dressed in two-coloured, or even multi-coloured combinations of various materials. Later, when she became a psychiatrist, when my father had a reasonable income, grandmother Ana continued to sew for my mother and myself, still in various combinations, twisting the material from left to right, turning it over innumerable times before cutting it out, so as to get as much as possible out of it. Between the two wars, my grandmother Ana went by train from Split to Belgrade, because at the time there were fashion magazines in Belgrade, while there probably weren't any in Split, in Split there was fascism. Had she lived in other circumstances, in another age, I am convinced that my grandmother Ana would have become our own Coco Chanel, perhaps even more famous, perhaps even better. But it was as it was, unjust and sad.

My mother was called Timea but according to some Catholic calendar, she should have been christened Katica.

I was accepted into the Split branch of SKOJ, the League of Communist Youth in June 1941. In Zagreb I had the conspirators' name Katica. In a shoe shop on a small square, I was given ankle-boots 'so as to move around Zagreb more easily'. In a Dalmatian bag over my shoulder the details of people joining the Partisans travelled with me and ended up at 24 Medvedgradska Street, where I entered them into a register. I was supposed to look elegant and unobtrusive, so I exchanged the ankle-boots for white shoes. I changed my hairstyle and tied plaits over my head.

In the hall of the Anatomical Institute, armed Ustasha students, who were ostensibly studying, followed our movements…

My grandmother Ana hated the name Katica and who knows from where she unearthed Timea. For a long time, I thought that Timea came from the Latin *timeo, timere* which could have been translated as Bojana.[12] Then in a small Hungarian village, at a fair, I saw that name written on demijohns for wine. So I concluded that it could be Hungarian, that it could in fact be an ordinary Hungarian village name, and not one with a secret Latin origin, although my family had no connection whatever with Hungary.

When you lose your mother and you are not yet very old, for years afterwards you scrabble about through what your mother left behind her, what was dragged out and then lost through moving house, marriages, divorces, births, because that's what happens, things are dragged out, lost and thrown away. You look for answers to questions that always surface too late. Too late. Like that school exercise book from 1937 that emerged twenty years after my mother's death. The war (this new one) was still going on, Sara and I had already left Belgrade and that notebook came with us to Rijeka. It was only then that I saw that the notes and rules printed in it were in the Cyrillic script, while everything else was, as it were, trilingual. It used the Serbian terms for 'chemistry' and 'history', the seal was half in the Latin script, half in Cyrillic, and the language being learned was called Serbo-Croato-Slovene. The marks were, of course, written in a fine Latin hand, with a pen, with thin and thick lines, the way we were taught in socialist times after the war, except that then calligraphy with thin and thick lines was barely possible as we wrote in chalk on little black slates, because there were no exercise books. There were no brightly coloured, shiny balls either, just rag balls, or marbles, those wonderful glass marbles each of which resembled the most beautiful imaginable artificial eye. There were only clay clumps, untreated, unsmoothed, almost angular, but I was the master, the best marble-player because I aimed faultlessly, standing up, from a height.

---

12 *Bojana* is a Croatian girl's name. The verb *bojati se* means 'to fear', hence the connection with *timeo*. {Translator's note}

Now I'd like to ask someone: was that breaking the rules, to write the marks in Latin script if the textbook was printed in Cyrillic? My mother's little book is in Rijeka and I am in Toronto, so I can't check the details: the coat of arms, the seal, the list of subjects, the marks. At the time I found the little book, during and after this war, various documents were beginning to surface from my friends' attics: their parents' university degree certificates, birth and marriage certificates, some from Zagreb, some from Split, all from the time of the Kingdom of Serbs, Croats and Slovenes, and all in the Cyrillic script. That set me thinking. All in all, throughout the whole of this last war, I've been thoughtful. How could I have known such things earlier, I who was born and brought up in the new Yugoslavia, when they were not spoken of, when there were more important tasks? You had to become a pioneer, then join a youth brigade and go to work camps, and read first Maksim Gorky, then Dobrica Ćosić (he didn't thrill us as a writer, but you couldn't so much as think that, let alone say it), you had to learn Marxism, then acquire a mac and ballet pumps and a bobbled twinset and velveteen skirt that didn't crush and – you had to fall in love. My father was also occupied, he was building the country and socialism (often in his own way which sometimes displeased the Party and Ranković[13] so much that my father was occasionally left without membership, without a job and without pay). My mother was completing her medical studies with various specialisations, she painted rooms, lacquered parquet, sewed curtains, knitted jumpers and attended parents' evenings. There was no time for looking backwards. The age was imbued with collective optimism, we were all looking towards a better tomorrow, there on the horizon.

For a long time, the main street in Rovinj was called 'Belgrade Street' and the only little cinema in Rovinj was called the 'Belgrade

---

13 Aleksandar Ranković, 1909–1983, was a Yugoslav communist politician, considered to be one of the most powerful men in Yugoslavia after Josip Broz Tito.

Cinema', but I didn't get upset because a lot of things in Yugoslavia outside Belgrade were called that. Only later (that was before this war, Tito was still alive) when the old name 'Carera' was restored to the main street in Rovinj, and when some holiday-home owners started to protest out loud, it was only when I heard a clerk at a post office counter say 'grazie' and not 'hvala' to a customer and the customer went berserk: Don't you grazie me, this isn't Italy, this is Yugoslavia! It was only then that I began to think. To notice all kinds of apparently little things.[14]

Between 1945 and 1975 it was not unusual for so-called 'little people' to write letters to Tito, believing that he would reply to them individually. As though Tito didn't have anything more important to do. Little people are called citizens. In that post-war period the citizens still believed in their citizens' rights. That's why they wrote letters to Tito.

So, I considered it my duty to report the truth, and you judge, Comrade President, the depths to which those Party leaders in the Poreč-Buzet district, have sunk in the recent electoral battle, slandering myself and my two sons as traitors and fascists, just because my son Boris agreed to the wish and request from a certain number of his acquaintances and friends that, in addition to the official candidate for delegate to the National Assembly, Josip Šestan, he too should put his name forward.

Because of the mud-slinging and persecution on the part of various Party leaders, during the period from the Liberation until 1948, many decent Istrians were inclined to opt for Italy, which is why the Central

---

14 After this war, in idle moments, and whenever I find myself in Rovinj at the post office, I remember the gentleman who had understood Yugoslavia so badly, and I wondered where he was now: in Pale? Had he been near Vukovar in 1992? Had he, like the writer Antonije Isaković sold his Adriatic holiday home in time, or maybe he had a foreign passport and now came to Rovinj quietly, almost secretly, and, instead of shouting at post office employees, now whispered all over the place?

Committee of the Communist Party of Croatia was obliged to intervene.
I am not suggesting that the Istrians are today inclined towards Italy, but
I do maintain that the behaviour of the afore-mentioned Party func-
tionaries in Poreč and Buzet, there, on the border, is worrying and will
do no good to either the Communist Party or democracy, and account
should be taken of their behaviour, and I most sincerely beg you to do
so, Comrade President.

Nowadays the citizens on the territory of the former Yugoslavia
have scant belief in the power of citizens' rights but they still write
letters to their various presidents. The less they believe in the power
of their citizens' rights, the more citizens on the territory of former
Yugoslavia believe in God. Over the last fifty years, citizenship has
coagulated and compressed and finally hardened. Today what we
have is a turd of citizenship.

In the course of the last four years, Sara and I have undergone
three migrations. A lot of books have been written about migration,
about leaving one's country, about exile, some very stupid, propaganda, some very intelligent. But all those books state clearly that
migration is both dying and being born, that it is a very complex
phenomenon, hard to comprehend for anyone who has not experienced it. Our arrival in Rijeka from Belgrade, where I had spent
forty years of my life and Sara almost all nine of hers, did not differ
fundamentally from our arrival in Toronto. In a way, arriving in
Toronto was more painless at least as far as the language went. Sara
learned the English words for various terms when it had been
harder for her to learn that certain Croatian words differed from
Serbian, although the language was essentially the same. In Toronto,
my accent was charming, because my accent in English was not
that recognisably a hard, Balkan one, so people asked me whether
I was perhaps French or, heaven forbid, a New Yorker. In Rijeka,

I was suspect as soon as I opened my mouth. At least to start with. While others chatted, I absorbed the new intonation, expressions, new words, old words, at home I repeated it all out loud and so learned a language that would make my presence in my own country legitimate.

But because of that I now know Croatian very well, just as I had learned Serbian very well when I lived over there, in Belgrade. I can write etymologically as well if needed. I know the dialects, I even know the chakavian dialect, which many great Croats don't know. After less than a year of living in Rijeka, Sara came top in Croatian in her class. We are adaptable, the two of us.

Each time I come back to Croatia, I see that it is not the Croatia I left, that I am not the person who left. Today, every lengthy departure from Croatia promises a still more difficult return, an ever more remote chance of establishing a firm, tenuously secure basis for living. Today, when I leave, I no longer know who I shall find alive when I come back.

My father, for instance. Over recent years my father has softened. My father's meekness found me unprepared, because now, when I could resolve some important things from the past with him, he has been reduced. I experience this softness of my father's, his fear of the final farewell, as a betrayal. As travesty.

Before every parting, my father lays out on the kitchen table old letters, photos, newspaper cuttings, political tracts. He brings them out and shows me what I have seen innumerable times, what I remember clearly, because what my father lays out in front of me are in fact the mementos of a past life that has marked our whole family. He brings them out, shuffling to and from the old chest, in which he keeps all of that locked up, through the half-dark hall, to the kitchen table. He takes things out and gives them to me. Photographs of my mother. My letters to him. Printed articles, reviews, stories with his or my signature at the end. I am bemused, upset and angry. My father was a politically very committed man, with relatively little time for my brother, my sister and me. I imagine him in some moments of solitude known only to him, cutting out my articles and sticking them into a scrapbook and so finding a way to spend time with me. Now he's giving all that back.

Once my father used to fill those old drawers with chocolate, key rings, badges, notebooks, little decorative figures made of ivory, miniatures by famous painters, the occasional gold bracelet or ring, ostrich eggs, his collection of stamps. Now there's nothing left. It has all been given away. The stamps, at decently separate intervals, he gives to Sara. She tries to enter the world of collectors. My father is saying goodbye. Clearing up after him.

31st August 1996, another 'cleansing', one more step towards disappearance. My father brings out my grandfather's letter to Tito. The letter ends:

Death to fascism – freedom to the people.
Edo Radan
To Comrade Josip Broz Tito,
Marshal of Yugoslavia and President of the Republic, Belgrade
Opatija, 5.xii. 1953.
95 Maršal Tito Street

Of course, Tito didn't reply to my grandfather. The Party replied to my father by punishing him.

Forty years later, I'm standing in Maršal Tito street in Opatija, surprised that the street still exists. I'm standing in front of number 95; it too exists. The large red house is a ruin, with a garden in which in 1953 I picked ripe tomatoes and thrust them secretly into my mouth, because they were being kept to make salsa. The garden is overgrown with weeds. Below the garden there used to be sea, I can't go and check, because some unknown people are living here. I show Sara and talk, it's all remote and uninteresting to her. I am in fact settling my accounts, she has not yet even begun hers. The apartment in this house was not given to my grandfather by either the Party or our struggle, instead he received the proceeds of the sale of my late grandmother's property. And into the property purchased with the proceeds of my late grandmother, the mother of my father, Boris Radan, my grandfather brought a new wife, far younger than himself, and her two children. The son was good and he died, the daughter was not good. My grandfather's new wife later exchanged that apartment for another which he gave to his spiteful daughter and sent my grandfather to a different village, to the property of his late wife, where there was neither water nor a toilet. There my grandfather lived, for the most part alone, burying the burned pans in which he cooked his little meals in the garden, because he was afraid that the new young wife would be angry when she came on one of her short visits. At this property, my grandfather raised bees (later they too disappeared), strawberries and grapes (they're not there anymore either), grapes for a litre of Malvazija wine which he mixed every day with honey and drank. My brother, sister and I came in the summer to watch the way that honey was extracted and grandfather kept hams for his sons which he would not let us near (the hams). When my grandfather died, my father and his brother sold that house. There, in that Istrian village house, strangers live now. There was one other house, in Pazin. That's where my father and my uncle were born. Today it's Pazin's administrative building. We've got nothing anymore. No houses. Nothing was taken from us, nothing was nationalised. There's nothing to be given back to anyone. My family sold their properties for a song because they were embarrassed to own property. It was not socialist to own property. It wasn't in the Party spirit. We had to be equal. We had to be poor, because that meant being honest. My brother, sister and I grew up like real proletarians. Our socks were full of holes at the heel and the elastic round our ankles had given out, so our socks dragged under the soles of our feet. That can be most annoying and it gives you blisters. Like real proletarians, we also developed small problems with our lungs, my brother, my sister and I. Later we were expected to be proud of that. The medication for tuberculosis was sold in huge dark brown jars. We weren't allowed to spend time with the children of the Americans who lived opposite and who had a real little swimming pool in their garden, and it was very hot and at the time we already knew English and a lot of American children's songs and rhymes by heart. Their children were capitalists (while we were proletarians), their pool and chocolate were capitalist propaganda, and if we visited them, we would arouse great suspicion with the Captain 1st Class who lived above us and stank of sauerkraut. Fifteen years later, at the end of the nineteen-sixties, that rule was still valid: you shouldn't go the American Reading Room, or the British Council – they were recruiting our young people for their capitalist West. I mention this only so that it shouldn't be forgotten. Nowadays many people have become forgetful. These are just gleanings, there is still plenty more.

In fact, my father wasn't convenient for the Party. He was forever quarrelling with it, just as he quarrelled all the time with me, only I was little and I had no power, while the Party was big and stern and dangerously strong. That Party betrayed my father on several occasions, while I (I hope) never did. That Party punished my father and threw him out of its ranks, after which he wrote complaints to the Control Commissions of the Central Committee of the Communist Party of Croatia and Yugoslavia, the Verification

Commissions of the Federal National Assembly,[15] to committees, and even to Tito (like my grandfather, my father too let himself be caught in that trap), while we lived off the sale of family jewels, occasionally horsemeat but that was already a feast day. We wore shabby old clothing that emigrés sent us from America,[16] smeared with jam so that the customs officers didn't confiscate it. Today, in Toronto, my daughter and I are again wearing second-hand clothes which we buy for a dollar or two in Salvation Army stores. The circle has been completely closed. In fifty years, my family has not made much progress.

We are a literate family. My mother wrote as well, but not letters, memoirs and diaries.

Split, 11 April 1941
Listening to enemy radio stations is strictly forbidden. A decree has been passed for windows to be blacked out. The janitor Mate is a cleric and great supporter of the struggle against communism.

---

15 In connection with the same elections for the national assembly of the Federal National Republic of Yugoslavia, held in the Poreč-Buzet District in November 1953, in connection with which my grandfather wrote to Tito, my father wrote to the Assembly. The process dragged on for more than three years, before my father's complaint finally reached the Central Committee of the Communist Party of Yugoslavia. There they must have revoked his punishments, because in 1957 he was sent with the diplomatic service to Egypt, just when war broke out there. Whether as a reward or a punishment, I don't know. Later, when he was again complaining about Ranković, they punished him again, and he appealed again, and they sent him, again I don't know whether it was a punishment or a reward – to the Sudan.

16 Lujo and Zlata Goranin sent most. Lujo played the accordion and sang nostalgic songs from the old country.

Split, 12 April 1941

Boris[17] writes from Zagreb that the trams aren't running. On the corner of Ljubljanska street and Ilica, he ran into German tanks. He watched an old Ford filled with supporters of Josip Frank coming from Jurišićeva street onto Jelačićev square. He says Savska street is full. He says he watched Germans also arriving on the square and well-dressed girls throwing flowers and oranges around their cars.

Split, 13 April 1941

Tonight we listened to Radio Moscow. The whole broadcast in Croatian was taken up with the story of a girl, Maria Demchenko, who had grown a turnip the size of a watermelon.

Split, 15 April 1941

Boris writes: 'At the telephone exchange in the printers' a German appeared, a chemistry student. He adores the cake shops in Zagreb and keeps talking about them. He says: you can buy a mountain of cakes very cheaply. He likes cream buns with extra cream best of all.

A decree has been published that anyone who has been in uniform must register at the collection camp for prisoners. We hit on the idea, we who at the time had the good fortune to be 'pure-blooded' Croats, of going to the Germans and vouching for our colleagues in uniform.

Antun told me: 'All Serbs should be exterminated, not saved.' Vijeko was even more vehement. As we parted, he didn't want to offer his hand to his colleagues. He said that 'serbische Untermensch' should perish. I saw him in a tram making old Jewish people get up, shouting that as long as there was one Aryan standing, Jewish trash must give up their seats.'

---

17 My mother's brother, my uncle, later a journalist on the Croatian newspaper, *Slobodna Dalmacija*. He died of a heart attack, watching a boxing match on television. He was 54.

Split, 26 April 1941

Boris writes that they haven't swum at Lake Jarun for a long time because agents were milling around them. 'In Karlovac, on 22 April, the city police brought in a decision limiting movement around the town for Jews and determining where they could live. According to that decision the Jews had to move out of the centre of the town at the latest by 1st July. I'm getting ready to go to Zagreb. Registration for the University has begun.'

But my mother didn't let herself be deceived. She had an enormous belly (I was inside it) when the Party told her that she had to build the Šamac-Sarajevo railway. She told the Party that for her the Party could take (perhaps) fourth but never first place, after her children, her husband, her homeland.

Today my mother can't see how wise she was not to have gone to build the Šamac-Sarajevo railway, because neither she nor the railway now exist and from this distance, I can't confirm who it was who dug it up in this new war, who would use it in future and on whose territory it would lie.

Today a lot of people from those days are dead, but their children are still alive. Today the descendants of Ustashas and the descendants of Partisans sit together and chat. And that's all right. And they argue. And justify themselves in the name of their fathers. In various ways. It's awkward that the descendants of Ustashas (and the Ustashas themselves) left Croatia earlier, while the descendants of Partisans are leaving only now. (There are almost no Partisans left; and those that have survived are too old to go anywhere, so they sit between their four walls or they are taken, like bears to a fair, to reunions commemorating victories over fascism, or called 'Committees for marking the 50th anniversary of the antifascist coalition in Europe and the world', and those committees contain some who did not remotely fight against fascism, quite the contrary.)

II

The 'Ellipsis' café. Excellent espresso. At the table next to mine sits a gentleman with false teeth. All the teeth in his artificial plate are equally rounded. They look wooden, they look dead. Dead teeth. Pale gums. As he speaks, the false teeth of the gentleman sitting at the next table are far too visible. The gentleman appears to be snarling. That gentleman has grey hair, hearing aids and a stick, although he doesn't limp. The gentleman with false teeth, hearing aids and a stick (the stick is expensive and classy), is wearing a beige suit of perfect cut. Over his shoulders he has laid a camelhair coat. The gentleman is talking (snarling) loudly. The gentleman is speaking Croatian and stressing the syllables wrongly. Since I am listening in, I gather that the gentleman is a successful businessman in Toronto. He says to his collocutor:

I condemn everyone who left Croatia after 1991.

I feel personally targeted.

When did you leave Croatia? His collocutor in jeans and trainers asks.

Thirty years ago.

Why didn't you go back, sir? Why didn't you go back in '91?

His collocutor has a nice face. I like nice faces. His collocutor has curly black hair. I like curly black hair.

You won't be accepted by the Croatian community here, you need to understand that, the gentleman clicks.

I haven't come here because of the Croatian community, says his collocutor.

You have to understand, our people here are very sensitive.

People in Croatia are very sensitive as well.

But you've got a Serbian accent.

And you speak in a completely uneducated way.

The businessman really did speak in a completely uneducated way, some bastard version of Croatian, a caricature mixture of Croatian dialects and English, fairly old-fashioned.[18] His collocutor, on the other hand, did not have a remotely Serbian accent, I was in an excellent position to judge, the collocutor spoke in a fluent, lively entirely contemporary way, stressing his words correctly. Only, he had a sing-song intonation, like a Spaniard or an Italian. In this linguistic question, my ear is infallible.

Another thing, the 'Spaniard' continued. *I've always been in opposition. Both to that former regime and to this one.*

There! The gentleman with a very discreet, almost transparent, hearing aid in his ear, brightened up. *That shows you are a real Croat.*

I'm Konrad Koše.

Then they parted. The Canadian Croat with the *kamelhaar* coat hanging casually from his shoulders showed Konrad Koše the two rows of his expensive teeth, while Konrad Koše showed him nothing.

---

18 In the Domobran or Home Guard Royal Hungaro-Croatian Artillery drill manual …, the legalized bilingual status of the Hungarian-Croatian Agreement of 1868 required that previously established terms should be replaced by a language of command abounding in monstrous Germanisms and Hungarianisms, which acquired the significance of convention, so that it did not offend anyone's ear, the way today the recent caricature of deformed neologisms, which appear as shadows of an already vanished era that prided itself on the false ornamental epithet: 'la belle epoque' …"

Translator's note: here the author lists a series of colourful terms and constructions identified by the Croatian writer Miroslav Krleža: *Djetinjstvo i drugi zapisi*, Sabrana djela Miroslava Krleže, vol.. 27, pp. 83-86, Zora, Zagreb, 1972. For more on the Croatian language, see: Stanko Lasić: Krležologija, Miroslav Krleža i Nezavisna Država Hrvatska (10.4.1941. – 8.5.1945.), Globus, Zagreb 1989, vol.3, pp. 183-238.

In Toronto it's not hard to come across emigrés like this: malicious, narrow-minded, rigid. Emigrés who do not know how to laugh unless they are with their cloned copies, paranoid emigrés, vigilantes, dangerous emigrés. Such people check up on every new arrival from Croatia, they have a network of conspiratorial channels, those emigrés are worse than the departed UDBA, the Yugoslav Secret Police.[19]

Konrad Koše was born in Zagreb, in the same hospital where I was born seven years later. Konrad Koše was born in 1939, on the eve of the war. Konrad Koše's father was an excellent chess-player and an average Ustasha, while Konrad Koše was an average basketball player and a good painter. There were some chess players in my family as well. After fifty or so years, maybe it's no longer crucial that Konrad Koše's father, Albert Koše, as a chess-player and secretary, was subordinate to a certain Mirko Magdić, the Ustasha responsible for 'the whole chess-playing organisation' in the Independent State of Croatia. In addition to persecuting, killing and slaughtering Jews, Serbs, Gypsies, anti-fascists and communists, the Ustashas (like other citizens for that matter) played chess and, in general, led a varied social and cultural life.[20] I presume that there is a scientifically

---

19 A woman's voice telephones me, in Croatian: I'm Suzana Lukić. What sort of classes are they at the University? What textbook do you use? We've got beginners and intermediate. Your Croatian seems too good for either, I say. Ask Professor B. about the textbook. But you don't speak Croatian at all. And who are you anyway, to be teaching at the University. You'll be hearing from me!?!

20 So, for example, in April 1941, the big Croatian State Theatre had in its repertoire the 'reprised' production of Puccini's *Manon Lescault*, with 'a completely new distribution of the main roles', Gundulić's *Dubravka* and Bizet's *Carmen*. The small Croatian State Theatre was playing Eugène Scribe's comedy *A Glass of Water*, then a play by Stjepan Šantić, *Golden Fields*, and Kleist's 'cheerful play' *The Broken Jug*. In the cinemas, the *Central, Croatia, Urania, Union, Trešnjevka, Tomislav, Grič, Rex* and so on, a less demanding audience could be entertained by the film *To the Homeland (Mein Mann will in die Heimat)*, with the prelude *The Bombing of Serbia*, then 'the great musical film' *The Symphony of Life*, or

based typology of human characters in which at least a small place is devoted to the 'chess-player type' who neither runs nor jumps, who doesn't swim or fly, who doesn't use any props, no balls, or sticks, or rackets, but just sits and stares in front of him, perfectly concentrated on devising tactics of attack and defence, who is in fact waging a war, which cannot be seen from outside. I would be able to find at least fifty books on that topic in the Robarts University Library, but I don't have time. My father, for instance, was an excellent chess player. Today, when he no longer has any social status and no political power, he plays far less and does more crosswords. My grandfather (the one who wrote letters to Tito) also played chess. As did my brother. And my cousin and one (just one) lover of mine. All of them, my father and my brother and my grandfather, and my uncle and my cousin and my lover, all tried to draw me into that conspiratorial game, that game with no élan, no joy, no loudness, but it didn't work.

The Queen of Czardas, with the latest war journal 'War in the Balkans'. From 6 pm Lika lamb kebabs were served at the restaurant DRAGO HRANILOVIĆ, at 9 Vlaška Street; reservations could be made by telephone 22-189. Business at the Markovski fair, in April 1941, was on the other hand bad, because, as the newspapers reported 'it rained'. But veal was sought after, while, because of high prices business in the Pork Department was poor. At the end of April 1941, 'The theatre was renovated according to the intentions of the Leader, the Poglavnik, with the clear principles of the Deputy' so that 'Before the time decreed for the oath of membership of the Croatian State Theatre to the Leader and Independent State of Croatia, the whole membership gathered on the stage. The background of the stage was decorated with greenery and a symbolic representation of the restored State of Croatia and a large image of the Leader, wrapped in the Croatian state flag. Before the oath was declared the previous Manager FREUDENREICH (my capitals) took his leave from the members and thanked them for their cooperation … The new manager, Professor Žanko stressed that the formal giving of the oath reflected the penetration of new ideas and facts into the conscience of every individual and announced impending reforms in the membership and programme of the theatre … In the 'Small Ads', under 'Men seeking work', it was possible to read that the Management was being taken over by Aryans with first-class references.

When Mirko Magdić, the Ustasha's commissioner for the 'whole organisation of chess' in the Independent State of Croatia (in some people's memory a very ambitious man who aspired to a career without any scruples), when, therefore Mirko Magdić went haywire and drove all the chess-players in Zagreb to choose: either they would take part in matches or they would be sent to concentration camps, something rebelled in Albert Koše. At an international competition in Slovakia, in the middle of 1941, he renounced his obedience to his superior Mirko Magdić and, with the help of a Slovak officer (a mediocre chess-player), he succeeded in crossing through France to England and from there, in 1945, to Brazil.

Zagreb, 7th July 1941
At the Red Cross they had organised a welcome for the Slovenes who had been moved out of their homes by the Germans. The first transport arrived. In it were old and young, men and women. We shared tea and cigarettes. The people came out of the wagon under German bayonets.

In Vončina Street I met the carpenter Baldy. He was being led away, covered in blood, by agents. He winked.

Mrs Koše, née Weiss, remained in Zagreb, with two young children, Irma (5) and Konrad (2). Mrs Koše, née Weiss, was not related to Deneš Vajs, in whose apartment at 10 Solovljeva Street illegal meetings of the Communist Party of Croatia were held, and whose two daughters have been living in the USA for more than twenty years now.[21] Because, if she had had any connection with Deneš Vajs,

---

21 Deneš Vajs died in the nineteen-eighties in one of the better retirement homes in Zagreb. He was of short stature, round and good. When my mother died, Deneš's wife Dana (a head taller than her husband, with eyes the blue of the ocean), travelled with Deneš from Zagreb, threw herself onto Timea's bed, hugged her pillow and whispered something into it for a long time, weeping. It seems that the two of them had their secrets, little wicked plans, unrealised.

Mrs Koše might not have been obliged to do what she did, because perhaps Deneš Vajs would have helped her.

Ten of them. As a reprisal for the death of Tiljak[22]. Posters everywhere.

Dr. Božidar Adžija

Prof. Ognjen Prica

Dr. Ivo Kuhn

Prof. Zvonimir Richtman

Alfred Bergman, about to graduate in agronomy

Sigismund Kraus, bank clerk

Otokar Keršovani, journalist

Ivan Korski, Engineer

Montenegrin, worker[23]

The caretaker at the Red Cross gets blankets, sheets and towels for us. There are arrests every day.

My aunt from Sarajevo fried veal cutlets in breadcrumbs, a mountain of veal cutlets, for those who had come to my mother's funeral from far away. Soon after that, Dana 'partizanka' also died, of ovarian cancer.

22 Ljudevit Tiljak, police agent, for many years the right-hand man of the notorious chief of the Belgrade Glavnjača prison camp, Kosmajac. In the middle of 1941, the Gestapo appointed him to the Ustasha police in Zagreb. He had an office in Đorđićeva Street. He used to leave the building always at a couple of minutes past 1pm, usually with a hat in his hand. He was bald. He had enormous experience in the struggle against Yugoslav communists. He had an excellent memory. He had a brother who was an aviator who lived on Ribnjak Street.

23 Five recognisably German surnames, possibly Jewish. I don't know whether later, in the new Yugoslavia, those recognisably German surnames, possibly Jewish, acquired streets (albeit narrow and short), or whether any firm or institution was named after them, I don't know. I could check that in the Robarts library as well, find a map of Zagreb. I don't know how things are now in the Republic of Croatia, whether (if they did exist) those streets have since been taken from them? The Robarts doesn't yet have a new map of Zagreb.

Irma and Konrad were cared for by their grandmother, while Zlata Koše went every morning to the State Mortgage Bank, renamed the State Credit Authority in 1941, where she worked as a counter clerk, receiving and paying out cash.

Zagreb, 13 July 1941.

Currency changed to 'kunas'. A lot of cash desks at counters.

Payment of cash for Jews, Serbs and former ministers banned. They give out only 500 kunas for a week.

The Rosenberger sisters retype the history of the bank. They have 'Underwood' typewriters. They wear yellow ribbons.

Agents in the bank arrested Micika Glasenhard.

Toothache. In Dr Hiršl's clinic, I found a dentist from the Ustasha board.

When the raids began after which her colleague Nada Hajligštajn[24] was arrested and then murdered, Mrs Koše, alone and unprotected, walked, one sunny July morning in 1941, to number 4 Zvonimirova Street which then housed the Ustasha Surveillance Service, the so-called UNS. After she had signed her loyalty to the Independent State of Croatia, she expressed her desire to work as an ordinary little secretary in that surveillance service or, perhaps, in an office with the police in Petrinjska or Đorđićeva Street or, if there was no position there either, perhaps in the prison at 9 Račkoga Street, perhaps at the Holy Spirit Hospital, perhaps at the War Court in Nova Ves, anywhere, just to leave the bank.

Konrad Koše will never discover whether his mother decided on this desperate step on the basis of her own deliberations or the

---

24 Among the Zagreb illegals the word was that Nada Hajligštajn and later the Baković sisters were betrayed by the arrested activists Milan Hupert and Ankica Sertić-Cincipinka.

advice that her husband Albert was still at that time sending in letters from Paris. He will never know whether his mother, Zlata Koše, née Weiss, was a devoted employee of the Ustasha police (where they, nevertheless, found her a job in the Archive) and, by denouncing her acquaintances and friends from as early as her primary school days, she succeeded (thanks to small rewards in the form of chocolate, oranges and an occasional pay rise), throughout the four difficult years of war, in feeding him, his sister and his grandmother Ilza.

Konrad Koše would wonder whether his mother had, perhaps, worked for the communists by passing on confidential data by means of secret channels, from that apparently insignificant cellar Archive. Konrad Koše would never really know why his parents had in fact divorced, was it in Albert's case really because of chess, and with Zlata was her maiden name of Weiss perhaps decisive. What is worst is that I shall never know either. I shall never know whether Zlata Koše had a role in the arrest of my mother, Timea-Katica, then a medical student; did she have any connection with the Ustasha agent Marija Osek, an employee of the Zagreb tram company, thanks to whom fourteen young people were captured, of whom twelve were tortured and killed, because Marija Osek herself was long since gone – she was liquidated by the communists after the liberation. I shall not know whether Zlata Koše had filed the case of the Baković sisters away in 'her' file in the police station in Petrinjska.

Zagreb, 3rd October 1941
Called into Zdenka and Rajka Baković's newsagent's in Nikolićeva Street. (Contact point for couriers.)

Zagreb, 7th December 1941
The Rosenberger sisters have been dismissed from their jobs. They won't join the Partisans. They can't leave their mother.

Zagreb, 21st December 1941

Went to the cinema: 'The Thief of Baghdad'. Old film, 1924, with Douglas Fairbanks in the main role. Called at the newsagents. Something has happened. A man with a little black moustache was standing beside Zdenka at the counter. Instead of 'hello', I said 'Good evening'. Zdenka said 'Madam'.

She had swollen hands. In the street I met Hupert. He already knew that there was an agent in the shop. A security lapse, in other words.

Zagreb, 1st January 1942

A note in the paper about the death of Zdenka and Rajka Baković. Ana told me that they had been beaten up at night but spent the day in the shop in case they might betray someone. Zdenka threw herself from the third floor of the Ustasha police station. Hupert and Cincipinka have been caught and are 'talking'.

Zagreb, 9th January 1942

I rang the bell at the Rosenberger sisters' house for a long time. No one opened the door. I used the key they had given me. The apartment was empty. The beds unmade. As though they had been picked up in the middle of the night.

Zagreb, 13th January 1942

All four Filipović sisters arrested.

Zagreb, 15th January 1942

Frosted windows. Mother is making brown roux soup. I went to the shop with vouchers for bread.

So, I shall never know whether Zlata Koše filed the case of the Baković sisters, the case of the Rosenberger sisters or the case of my mother in 'her' files at the police station in Petrinjska street. But I would wonder, I would wonder about that and a lot else while nearly fifty years later, in Toronto, Konrad Koše, her son, talked to me about Modigliani, about Lautrec, about Paris once and now, as he made little foamy pancakes, topped with 'amaretto di sarono' on cold Canadian nights.

Zagreb, 27th August 1942
A search warrant has been issued for the cobbler Ivo throughout Zagreb.[25]
In the train I met a group of Zagreb students on their way to their homes in Osijek. They're Jews.

Zagreb, 3rd September 1942
Vojo[26] *didn't come to the rendezvous. In the evening I discovered that he had been caught in front of the University Library and that he was already dead. They say that he had nails hammered into his joints.*

Zagreb, 21st September 1942
Vlado – code name Nose – came to the rendezvous. He needed shoes and has big feet. He was taken to the shoemaker Mlacović (an anti-fascist

---

25 Perhaps Ivan Šimecki? In the Robarts library there is no answer to such questions. But, in the Robarts library, the largest university library in Canada, there is a lot of information about cobblers who helped the Anti-fascist movement in Zagreb, between 1941 and 1945. I discovered that the illegals mostly used the premises of a certain Masnec, in Jurišićeva street; that the artisan shoemaker Ljudevit Blažičko had a shop in Mirogoj street, the cobbler Mance in Radićeva; the artisan Stipančić, in Ilica, opposite Gundulićeva; Franjo Podrugić, in Praška. It seems that there were a lot of cobblers in Zagreb. There were a lot of factories as well, especially of textiles.

26 Vojo Kovačević, member of the office of the Local Committee of the Communist Party of Zagreb. He was betrayed, according to my uncle's recollection, by the 'provocateur and informer Majerhold'.

from Istria), who fixed his old ones as best he could. He didn't charge for the favour.

Zagreb, 30th October 1942
'The Plough – Student magazine of the Croatian soil and man' is ever more aggressive.[27] *In the last issue, the editorial read: 'Croats may only be Croatophiles. Any other allegiance that crosses the boundaries of our shared commitments, is not only completely nonsensical but also absolutely harmful. So all contradictions can be manifested only within the borders of our national and state benefits. It is better that those borders should be narrower rather than wider, it is better that in establishing those borders we should be narrow-minded, rather than allow ourselves greater liberties.'*

After the liberation, Zlata Koše was left in peace. She went back to her job as a bank clerk, she worked in Trešnjevka and lived in Dubrava, so spent half the day in trams dragging plastic bags, in which there were always small bunches of celery sticks, carrots and parsley for soup. Her daughter Irma got a degree in chemistry, married and, there she is, still living in Zagreb, in Heinzelova street, looking after her grandchildren. When he graduated from the Academy of Art, in the middle of the nineteen-sixties, Konrad went to visit his father in Rio. In 1990, he came back to Zagreb, buried his mother Zlata and set up in her apartment a kind of branch of the Croatian Democratic Union (HDZ) and put on three one-man exhibitions. Then, realising his mistaken assessment of the political situation, probably a little ashamed, arrived in Toronto, at roughly

---

27 The editor-in-chief of the 'Student of the Croatian soil and man' was Ejub
Čengić. The Editorial Board was in Zagreb and the owner of the paper was the
Ustasha University Headquarters. The publisher purported to be the Society
of Croatian Academicians.

the same time as I did. In the 'Ellipsis' café, after the conversation with the gentleman businessman, our eyes met, and, as in romance fiction, we smiled at one another and our love affair, burdened with ideological-political, psychological-philosophical, intellectually and physically sadomasochistic disputes and showdowns, showdowns capriciously set up and sometimes pointless, burdened with obstacles in a multitude of variations – was able to begin.

New love affairs in late middle age are gruelling. The partners want to know all kinds of things about each other, everything that happened before they met. And there's usually a lot of it. The partners ask questions, constantly, they talk about the past, they describe, classify, compare, tidying both their own life and that of their new companion into historical, personal, professional, emotional pigeon-holes. How exhausting it is, how little it achieves.

I was caught in a trap. I began to be obsessed by the past of Konrad Koše and that of his family to such an extent that I forgot about Konrad. And he made wonderful pictures, he told Sara fairy tales, he laughed out loud, he took us to the lakes. I wondered, I have to say, how come the two of us had met in meridians so distant from the core of both our lives. How come the life of Konrad Koše, in individual episodes, was transformed into a copy of the life of his father Albert Koše, from whom he had parted so long ago, for whom he had longed for thirty years, to whom he had gone, only to leave him twenty years later because of the call of blood and soil. Konrad Koše had left a wife and two already grown children in Brazil, believing that, when he had painted his new, independent Croatia, the way he had dreamed it, he would go back for them. They were Brazilian, what would they do in Croatia? But I was looking for answers to questions that no one could have given me. Did his mother play a role in the arrest of mine? Who, actually, was his mother? Why did Albert Koše run away in 1941? My obsession took me to another time, among other people, on the other side of reason. I studied everything the Robarts Library held on the subject of the Croatian Democratic Party, the Communist Youth Organisation, the Communist Party, illegals in Zagreb from 1941 to 1945. In my imagination, wondering whether it was now only my imagination, I walked through the streets of my hometown in a time in which I hadn't been there. I got to know informers, Homeguard officers, the police 'experts' Šoprek and Šapinac, the Ustasha police officer Ivan Škunca, then Ivan Sertić, who had prepared the arrests of young people and communists. I followed the movements of Lojzika Praviček who worked in the 'Gaon' factory, in order to understand how she became an informer. I followed the courier and railway worker Mato Rendulić, who was arrested by the Ustashas and who 'grassed' on his friends, and who disappeared without trace after the war. I imagine Uvanović, head of the Independent State of Croatia's information service, issuing Cividini's orders, who had been beating people up even in Bedeković's time, and continued in the Jasenovac concentration camp. I see the Ustasha cut-throat Škelin in bed with his lover and later holding a child in his arms, singing to it. What kind of ditties is he singing? I see the agent and policeman Kanber beating my mother, her plaits undone; hitting her on the head and face, and her ear hurts and later in life she's afraid that she's going to get facial palsy and that she'll suffocate and in the end that's what happened to her, both the palsy, which distorted her lovely face incurably and the suffocation, which killed her.

In my imagination I visited the apartments in which the illegals hid, some of them still children, I visited the stores for sorting propaganda, antifascist material (the workers' bakery at 69 Maksimirska street, the Public Health Institute, the pasta factory at 34 Preradovićeva street, the nursery in Krajiška street …), I found out everything that could be found out from Canada about the organisations of cobblers, barbers (Pavišić from Mesnička street, Muharem Grozdanić, Ivan Mesner, Ivo Bogdan), especially barbers, because my grandfather, the communist, born in Zagorje, who adored Goethe, was a barber and he made wigs for the Split theatre. Then, tram workers: the cheery mountaineer and singing guitarist Buterin, and Živko Kovačević, then Stjepan Bubanić. Then tailors, especially tailors, because of my grandmother Ana, an experienced seamstress: Tomo Bahun, Mr Grah of 17 Krapinska street. I visited factories in the Zagreb of the Independent State of Croatia: the 'Higiea' cork factory; the 'Hardtmuth' pencil factory; the 'Derop' factory of paper goods (did it make coloured cups and plates for children's birthday celebrations in the Independent State of Croatia?); the 'Sil' stocking factory; the AEG factory; 'Singer'; 'Ventilator'; the 'Fussmann Brothers'.

(At 11 Ilica street, jewellers and watchmakers, I met Hilda Fussmann, née Krušić and watched her being chased by the Ustasha officer Godina); the oil factory; the 'Tiger' furrier's; the 'Zvono' woollen goods; the 'Vako' battery factory; the 'Zenit' lacemaker's; textile factories and weavers (they were the largest number): 'Grivičić', 'Hahn and Nettel', 'Roltex', 'Ivančica'; the furniture factory (owned by Josip Volarić); the 'Bor' co-operative; the 'Kaštel' factory of pharmaceutical products; 'Minerva' – Radio Zagreb, contact Roman Drausinger at 28 Petrinjska street; 'Rheinmetall' – the best calculating machines, Notter and Company, 5 Gundulićeva street; the 'Lim' tin factory (we used them, those tins, for years after the war, to carry pies and battered chicken on all our picnics, so that they didn't dry out); the largest dental laboratory run by Milan Čorko at 4/I Tkalčićeva street, that made modern dental prosthetics and bridges with the most up-to-date apparatus; the 'Inko' factory of laboratory apparatus (this is where Kazimnir Biloh made the detonators for blowing up the Main Post Office); the PAB, Privileged Agrarian Bank; the 'Luxor' cinema (*Wasser für Canitoga* with Hans Albers and *Romanze in Moll*, directed by Helmut Kautner); the undertakers, 29 Gajeva street – telephone 84-44, offers free funerals, 'Why burden your loved ones – in their most difficult hour – with difficult worries and expense. Think in good time of the last things!'

Then I embarked on studying the literature about the Croatian leader, Pavelić, Cardinal Stepinac, the Vatican. Metres and metres of paper, acres of titles emerged from the computerised catalogue in the Robarts Library: Hrvoje Matković, *Povijest Nezavisne Države Hrvatske* (*History of the Independent State of Croatia*), Zagreb, 1994; *Odmetnička zvierstva i pustošenja u Nezavisnoj Državi Hrvatskoj u prvim mjesecima života Hrvatske* (*Vicious reprisals and devastation in the Independent State of Croatia in the first months of its existence*), Zagreb, The Croatian Democratic Party, 1991; Vladimir Dedijer, *The Yugoslav Auschwitz and the Vatican*, Buffalo, New York, 1992; Vladimir Žerjavić, *Opsesije i megalomanije oko Jasenovca i Bleiburga* (*Obsessions and megalomania around Jasenovac and Bleiburg*), Zagreb, 1992; Egon Berger, *Četrdesetčetiri mjeseca u Jasenovcu* (*Forty-four months in Jasenovac*), Zagreb, 1966; Stella Alexander, *The Triple Myth: A Life of Archbishop Stepinac*, New York, 1987; Milan Bulajić, *Misija Vatikana u Nezavisnoj Državi Hrvatskoj* (*The Mission of the Vatican in the Independent State of Croatia*), Belgrade, 1994; Ivan Cvitković, *Ko je bio Alojzije Stepinac* (*Who was Alojzije Stepinac?*), Sarajevo, 1986; Annemarie Gruenfelder, *Beitrage zur Biographie von Kardinal Stepinac*, Vienna, 1982; A nameless Istrian, *Stepinac, un innocente condannato*, Vicenza, 1982; Father M. Raymond, *The Man For This Moment*, New York, 1971; Ivan Mužić, *Pavelić & Stepinac*, Split, 1991; Ivo Rojnica, *Susreti i doživljaji* (*Encounters and Experiences*), Munich: Knjižnica hrvatske revije, 1969-1983; Stella Alexander, *Church and State in Yugoslavia Since 1945*, Cambridge University Press, 1979; Bogdan Krizman, *Ante Pavelić i ustaše* (*Ante Pavelić and the Ustashas*), Zagreb, 1978; Marija

Kovačić, *Od Radića do Pavelića; Hrvatska u borbi za svoju samostalnost* (*From Radić to Pavelić, Croatia's fight for independence*), Munich, 1970; Petar Džadžić, *Nova ustaška država? Od Ante Starčevića do Pavelića i Tuđmana* (*A new Ustasha state? From Ante Starčević to Pavelić and Tuđman*), Belgrade, 1991. (Džadžić died soon after publication of his book); Jakov Blažević[28], *Mač a ne mir* (*The Sword, not Peace*), Zagreb, 1980; Vinko Nikolić (died 1997), *Stepinac mu je ime/ zbornik uspomena, svjedočanstava i dokumenata* (*His name is Stepinac. A collection of memoirs, witness statements and documents*), Zagreb, 1991; Ivan Krtalić, *Sukob s desnicom* (*Conflict with the Right*), Zagreb, 1989; Father Aleksa Benigar, *Alojzije Stepinac hrvatski Kardinal* (*Alojzije Stepinac, Croatian Cardinal*), Rome, 1975; *Vjekoslav Cvrlje, Vatikan u suvremenom svijetu* (*The Vatican in the Modern World*), Zagreb, 1980; Vjekoslav Cvrlje, *Vatikanska diplomacija* (*Vatican Diplomacy*), Zagreb, 1992. (with interest and naïve surprise I compare the views of the author of the first book with those of the author in his second book, concluding that they are in places absolutely contradictory, which – given that in 1980 the Socialist Federal Republic of Yugoslavia existed and in 1992 only the Republic of Croatia, should not have been a surprise); *Tajni dokumenti o odnosima Vatikana i ustaške NDH* (*Secret Documents about Relations between the Vatican and the Ustasha Independent State of Croatia*), Zagreb, 1952. There was no end to it. Then, daily, weekly and fortnightly newspapers, magazines, diaries. I dragged all that home and read, looked, compared, studied and went crazy. In the 'Croatian Nation' I found poems by Archbishop Šarić of Sarajevo, dedicated to the Leader;[29] I read letters from Cardinal Stepinac from 1925 written to his fiancée Marija Horvat; extracts from reports of the CIA from 1950 about the priest Krunoslav Draganović, then extracts from his diary.

---

28 Died in 1996 or 1997. History does not have much good to say about him.

29 Ante Pavelić. {Translator's note}

I learned that, despite being proclaimed a war criminal, in 1967 he appeared in Sarajevo (was he kidnapped?) and began to teach at the Theological Faculty, and died in Sarajevo in 1982. The more I read, the less I knew. No one was entirely innocent, no one was entirely guilty: not the cardinals, nor the bishops, nor the popes, nor the churches, nor the Vatican. Nor the communists. As the for the Ustasha 'truths', I read them too, but I didn't believe them. They all had their version of history. Those who had survived. The CIA had its truth as well. America and Great Britain their own.

I discovered a lot of secrets, a lot of combinations, dark, political, religious, ideological, personal, to do with chess; spying, double and triple secret agents from all camps, secret police involved in dirty activities. There was fascism, there was communism and the bugbears of communism. Now, there is, supposedly, none of that, and all the filth of those times has been swept under the carpet. It is here, it is all here, hidden, transformed into democracy, which is not that. Because, for instance, what is now sold as democracy is in fact levelling, in fact it is restriction, a great restriction that threatens a whole lot of small restrictions by the police for everyone who does not submit. You have only to set out to acquire an ordinary street cat in Canada, for things to become clear. You have only to try to overturn the senselessness of any, even the least important, law, to enter into an argument with a librarian, let's say, (and she can't possibly be right, not even remotely), to pull down the whole system onto your shoulders. Go into files out of which you never emerge. This modern world, its technology, its working class, out-classed, its people equally clean, equally fed, equally cheaply clothed, equally healthy (non-smokers and sportsmen), equally chronically tired and empty, with an equally 'high quality of life' (?!), equally (un)interested (in other countries and people) because they are a big family, a global village (I'm heartily sick of global villages, global people, global everything), with equally (false) rights, none of that has any connection with democracy. Denim is the greatest enemy of democracy. As, for that matter, bicycles are in China. 'Residential districts', sunshine districts, youth districts, teachers' districts, workers' districts, districts for the elderly, skyscrapers and – kibbutzes and collective farms. To attain perfection in the organisation of life. As God commands, so does democracy. And Big Brother is still here. He is multiplied in countless Little Brothers who conceal themselves in invisible information bases from where they monitor everything we do. Little Brothers follow us everywhere. While we stand at the checkout in a supermarket, even, they scan our faces and, on the basis of what we are buying, they conclude what we are like: whether we eat expensive or cheap food, greasy or non-greasy, whether we are diabetics, whether we have pets, how many people live round us, whether we invite guests, are invited out, how often, which films we watch, with whom (tickets are increasingly frequently bought on-line), what our income is, where our outgoings are spent. Orwell is naïve material these days.

After that, I moved into books about war crimes, books about searching for war criminals, and that searching has not yet been completed, while the war criminals have either already died, or they are over eighty, have prostate disease, sclerosis, Parkinsons and a great many grandchildren. I discovered that it was only in 1985 that Canada, for instance, began to undertake concrete steps to take them to court, while they, the war criminals, had been buying land, houses, restaurants for four decades already, some worked for the secret or federal police, and suffered from profound amnesia. Almost every day, the Daily papers *The Globe and Mail* and *The Toronto Star* include a little 'tale' about war crimes among us. In 1993, Deborah Lipstadt wrote *Denying the Holocaust: The Growing Assault on Truth and Memory*; 1995, James E. McKenzie: *War Criminals in Canada*; in 1994, Warren Kinsella published *Web of Hate*; 1993, Robert Brym: *Jews in Canada*. Fifty years have passed, in the West there was no communist censorship or reign of terror, but justice over these issues has not yet been completely realised. The 'truth' is still being revealed. How come?

In 1945 Kurt Meyer was accused of the murder of forty-one Canadian soldiers in the small German town of Aurich in June 1944. In January 1946 he was sentenced to life imprisonment. Through England, he was sent to a Canadian prison. In 1951, so that he could be closer to his family, he was transferred from a Canadian to a German prison. In 1954 he was released. He died on 21st December 1961, on his fifty-first birthday.

Wilhelm Mohnke was accused of having ordered, in 1940, near Dunkirk, the shooting of twenty British prisoners of war. He commanded troops that had, in 1945, in the German offensive in the Ardennes, killed seventy-two American prisoners of war. He was responsible for the murder of thirty-five Canadian prisoners in Normandy. In the last years of the war, he was promoted to SS-Brigadeführer (Major General). The Canadians searched for him, while he sat in Moscow for ten years, in the Lubyanka. He returned to Hamburg, without any pomp, in 1955. He became a prosperous businessman. In the course of the celebration of the fiftieth anniversary of D Day, in June 1994, Mohnke was eighty-three, the last living SS General, cultivating the garden round his little house in a suburb of Hamburg and going for short walks.

Jacques de Bernonville was the director of public order in the Lyon district and an immediate colleague of Klaus Barbier. Before the collapse of the Vichy regime, he fled to a Benedictine monastery, then moved to the USA, and, in 1947, dressed as a priest and with a false passport, he came to Quebec. In the same year, the French Supreme Court sentenced him, *in absentia*, to death. At that time Bernonville was working in a firm that sold powdered milk; he was protected by the Quebec nationalist right. He went to Brazil in 1951. Twenty years later, he was found dead in his flat in Rio de Janiero, his arms and legs bound. (Ask Koše whether he knows anything more about this.)

In the early nineteen-fifties, around two thousand Ukrainians, former soldiers of the Galician division, an exceptionally fanatical organisation of the Nazi regime, were allowed into Canada. The Canadian agricultural industry, the energy sector, forestry, were in full swing. Canada needed workers. Haralds Puntulis left Latvia before the communists came to power. From a refugee camp in Sweden, in 1948, he emigrated to Toronto. He was sentenced, *in absentia*, in 1965, in Riga. Accused, as the chief of police of the Fourth district, in Rezekne, along with five of his co-workers, of being responsible for the death of 5,128 Jews and 311 Gypsies, and of the deportation of around 5,000 people of non-Jewish descent to German camps, he was sentenced to death by firing squad. He died in 1982 in Toronto, of natural causes, in the arms of his wife Anna, in his nice redbrick house. He was seventy-three.

On the ninth of May 1939, a ship, the *St Louis* left Hamburg. Destination – Cuba. There were 937 people on board, for the most part Jews, the majority of whom had already spent time in concentration camps before Kristallnacht. The *St Louis* waited in the harbour to see whether the Cuban authorities would approve its passengers' entry into the country. Cuba refused. The ship, the *St Louis*, set off for Florida with the same aim. Florida did not accept the passengers. After that, it set off for Canada. The then Minister for Immigration Affairs, Frederic Blair,[30] also refused the request of the passengers on board the *St Louis*, for the most part Jews, for

---

30 A ferocious anti-Semite. He spoke openly of Jews as 'liars and cheats' who 'destroy' every country in which they settle. No milder than Blair were the then Canadian Prime Minister Mackenzie King and leading diplomat Vincent Massey.

entry into the country. Five weeks after it had set sail, the *St Louis* returned to Germany. In the meantime, Belgium, Holland, France and England offered asylum to Jews from Germany. Many from the ill-fated ship, also known as *The Wandering Jew*, then travelled to their new homes by train. 287 people settled in England. Of the 937 frantic and tormented people who had set off on the journey by sea, 907 returned. The others died of dysentery and other diseases, or they jumped off the deck in the harbours of their temporary stay, in the hope that, when they swam into the new country, it would accept them. Final tally: three quarters of those who had embarked for a better future on 9th May 1939 later disappeared in camps.

At the beginning of the nineteen-fifties large numbers of Slovaks also arrived in Canada. Among the roughly fifteen hundred arrivals at that time, there were some high-ranking officials of the notorious regime of Jozef Tiso which, in the aims and methods of its government reminds one irresistibly of that of the Croatian wartime leader, Pavelić. Forward for an independent Slovakia! (The sovereign state of Slovakia was proclaimed on 14th March 1939.) Jozef Tiso was a Catholic priest and the tally of his regime amounted to the extermination of 70,000 of the existing 90,000 Slovak Jews. In the nineteen-fifties, the Canadian authorities simply wiped that fact from their memories. Individual Slovaks arrived in Canada thanks to the Allied Secret Service, others with the blessing of the Catholic Church, such as, for instance, Karol Sidor.

Karol Sidor was the founder and first commander of Hlinka's Guards, the paramilitary formation of Hlinka's party. Andrej Hlinka died in 1938 and Jozef Tiso took his place. Sidor became one of Tiso's highest functionaries. He was reluctant to subordinate himself to the Nazi authorities, so Tiso sent him to Rome as the Slovak ambassador to the Vatican. He stayed there until the end of the war. At the end of the nineteen-forties, Pope Pius XII asked Canada to accept Sidor, and the then prime minister, Louis St Laurent, agreed to his request. Sidor died in 1953.

Karol Murin, Tiso's secretary for political questions, settled in Canada; as did Matus Cermak, the Slovak ambassador in Nazi Germany. Followed by Konstantin Culen, Tiso's minister for propaganda, and Ferdinand Durcansky, his foreign minister. No charges were ever brought against any of them.

In 1948, Joseph Kirschbaum, as a collaborator of the Nazi regime, was sentenced in Czechoslovakia, *in absentia*, to twenty years in prison. Born in 1913, he studied law in Bratislava. He wrote for a Fascist newspaper in Slovakia. A vehement Slovak nationalist. (He later wrote a book about the history of Slovakia.) In November 1938 he participated in negotiations in Berlin with Goering, seeking Nazi support for the proclamation of an independent Slovakia. Four months later, Tiso and Hitler signed a declaration of Slovak 'independence'. In 1942, Kirschbaum lost his position as general secretary of the Party. He was transferred to Switzerland to the post of Slovak chargé d'affaires. He stayed there till the end of the war, then went to Rome where he zealously helped Slovak exiles to secure visas for peaceful and safe democratic countries. He helped himself as well. With papers issued by the Vatican, he knocked on the door of the United States. The US said: you're not welcome, but Canada said: by all means. He landed in Halifax in 1949. Over the years, here and there newspapers printed stories about Kirschbaum's past, but none of that raised much dust. At the end of 1992, after five decades, Kirschbaum went to visit his homeland, his newborn independent Slovakia. He was eighty.

Not counting the 'interns', young German Jewish women, some 2,500, that Great Britain sent to Canada and who were kept for the duration of the war in camps, often alongside Nazi prisoners, between 1939 and 1945, Canada allowed altogether some five hundred Jews across its borders. Of all the western democracies,

Canada has the most shameful past when it comes to offering refuge to those fleeing from the madness of Nazism. Many Latin American countries accepted tens of thousands of Jews at that time. The United States, and even tiny Palestine, over a hundred thousand. Shanghai, the only place in the world which did not ask for an entry visa for Jews, took around 20,000 European Jews, mostly of German origin.

During the Second World War, Bulgaria protected its Jews: when the president of its parliament heard that the deportation of Jews was imminent, he went to the Patriarch and asked him to intervene. The Patriarch went to the Emperor and the Emperor summoned the German ambassador and so the Bulgarian Jews stayed in their own country. Denmark also saved its Jews. When the SS order came to say that all Jews in Denmark must wear a yellow ribbon, the majority of Danes pinned a yellow star to their chests. Including the king, as he rode his bicycle. Filip says that in Canada, until the middle of the nineteen-fifties, there was a quota for Jews to register at universities. So, now there are Jews here with two or more degrees, not remotely related, because they registered where there was space for them and not for courses that appealed to them. Dr Simson, an intern in Toronto, says that until the nineteen-seventies there were no Jewish psychiatrists or surgeons in the hospitals. Today Canada is cleansing itself, but doing so gradually and shamefully. That's being done on the whole by individuals and independent societies. At state level there has still been no official apology.

So, on Saturday 19th October 1996, Toronto saw the first night of the children's opera *Brundibar,* by the composer and conductor Hans Krasa (gassed in the chambers of Nazi Germany) and the librettist Adolf Hoffmeister. In addition to a small number of adults, the cast consisted of forty-three children aged between eight and thirteen. Why this particular children's opera?

Some forty kilometres north of Prague, there is a small town with around five thousand inhabitants and a pharmaceutical factory. The town has two stone forts and a prison. And four small ovens, but not baker's ovens, gas ovens, sited within the walls of a once intimate, almost chamber crematorium which nowadays, thankfully, serves only as a feature. The town was founded by Emperor Joseph II in 1780 in order to defend Prague from invaders from the north and in honour of his mother Maria Theresa he gave the town the name Terezin. It was a completely military, garrison town, so, in addition to the two forts and the prison, it had a few houses and a lot of huts.

In 1941, Hitler decided to donate a town to the Jews which he would make into a 'model ghetto'. Terezin caught his eye, he changed its name to Theresienstadt and transformed it into a rather different fortress from the former one – a fortress surrounded by barbed wire. The Nazis named this fortress 'Paradeisghetto'. They settled the Jewish intellectual elite of Central Europe there. The smaller fort was used as the police prison of the Prague Gestapo, ensuring its newly arrived inhabitants peaceful sleep and a happy future. The Nazi propaganda in connection with the settlement of Theresienstadt was like that of contemporary tourism. Brochures were printed and invitations splashed about for the 'beautiful health resort' on the banks of the Ohra and Laba with theatres, galleries and tea-shops, surrounded by lush orchards and gentle hills. Hundreds of Jews settled there and paid for 'apartments with lovely views'. The first inhabitants arrived on 24th November 1941 and the last were taken out, either dead or half-alive, in April 1945.

There were painters in Terezin, and they painted and exhibited, organising art exhibitions. And they taught the children in Theresienstadt to paint, and they hid those paintings and today 6,000 of their works hang in Terezin and tell appalling stories. There were doctors and philosophers and so lectures were held. There were journalists, so papers were printed. There were writers who told the children fairy tales which they didn't believe, because if they had, they would not have drawn those horrors.

Most of all, there were musicians. There were so many that it was possible to form two whole symphony orchestras that were able to perform at the same time every day. There were musicians in several chamber orchestras. Verdi's 'Requiem' was performed, attended by many SS functionaries, including Eichmann. There was a performance of Smetana's 'The Bartered Bride'. It's true that Mendelssohn's 'Elijah' had to be cancelled because the entire choir was suddenly sent to the gas chambers.

There were prominent conductors and composers in Theresienstadt. And of course, they conducted and composed. And that was how an operetta for children – 'Brundibar' – came into being in that 'health resort', in that 'paradise ghetto'.

'Little Floramye' is also an operetta, although it did not come into being in one of the Ustasha camps and, unlike a few little things that made Theresienstadt 'a piece of cake' compared to Jasenovac, which aren't at the moment relevant (those little things), 'Little Floramye' is relevant.

In the last three or four years, for the first time since the war the music composed in Theresienstadt, including 'Brundibar' ('Bumblebee'), is beginning to be played all over the world, as a kind of homage to the victims of Nazi-Fascism, and it was played in my neighbourhood, in Slovenia. (In Croatia there is still no chance of anything like that – in Croatia people play traditional peasant instruments, 'diple' and 'gusle', 'Jure and Boban' have been revived[31]

---

31 The Ustasha soldiers Jure Francetić and Rafael Boban are thought to be the authors of the Croatian marching song first used by the Ustashas, 'Evo zore, evo dana' (*Here comes the dawn, here comes the day*). It was written after the Black Legion's battle for Kupres in the summer of 1942. {Translator's note, based on Wikipedia.}

– on a state and parliamentary level – arms raised in a Fascist salute, and the dead, such as Rojnica, Šakić and company are politically rehabilitated, some here, some there.[32]

The last of the 55 productions performed in Theresienstadt took place in September 1944 (the operetta was first performed in 1942, in a Prague orphanage), because the entire ensemble had to leave suddenly by train to the east, to Poland, to Auschwitz. Most of them died there. John Freund, aged thirteen at the time, survived. In his Toronto apartment, he remembered:

Terezin was no ordinary town. Terezin was a transitional camp during the Holocaust; for its inhabitants, a place halfway to their final destination – the gas chamber. The buildings in the camp were in fact three-storey huts, each of which also had an attic. Monstrous buildings. Everything was crammed full and crowded – 50,000 people lived on one square kilometre.

Between 1941 and 1945, 140,000 deported Jews passed through Terezin, of whom more than 90,000 were later killed in other camps. Some people stayed in Theresienstadt for a couple of weeks, some for several months or even years. As a result of insupportably bad living conditions, more than 35,000 people died there. Around 16,000 people survived in Theresienstadt, including just a hundred and thirty-two out of 15,000 children.

The performance took place in one of the numerous attics, virtually in the dark. Of the two to three hundred present, many had to stand.

In 1944 a great restoration of Theresienstadt began. The inmates cleaned and repaired the streets, removing the rubbish and stench. The huts were painted different colours, in pastel shades, so that they would appear mild and demure. Flowers were planted, some so-called gardens dug. The Nazis opened shops and filled their

---

32 Ivo Rojnica, suspected Nazi war criminal; Dinko Šakić, concentration camp commander. {Translator's note}

shelves and windows with all kinds of fine little things for looking at. From the baker's came the aroma of warm bread, for smelling. The inmates built a music pavilion and a few new cafés in which they played music far into the night. The nurses were provided with new uniforms, new bed-linen and new patients. The really sick, in mind as well as body, were placed in the gas chambers of Auschwitz. Sweets were procured. Then fresh, new, healthy children were procured (and soon afterwards forever despatched), and the urchins, dirty and worn-out, were washed under showers of Zyklon B. And, of course, that all took place rousingly, accompanied by song. A small paradise was created.

Then at the beginning of June 1944 a film was shot. The film was called *The Führer Presents the Jews a Town* and it showed clearly that Theresienstadt was a little heaven.

Then on the 23rd June 1944, Hitler allowed functionaries of the International Red Cross into Theresienstadt and allocated Eichmann as their guide. The functionaries were delighted. In their report, they wrote that despite the war conditions, the Jews were living well in Theresienstadt. That they were treated humanely. And they cancelled their pre-arranged visit to Buchenwald.

Theresienstadt was the only Nazi concentration camp that functionaries of the International Red Cross ever visited.

Now let's pay a little visit to Jasenovac.

Jasenovac was also visited by various commissions, various functionaries of the International Red Cross and some journalists. Their guide was Luburić, and the visits were arranged by Pavelić. The journalists were trusted editors and writers of Nazi and Ustasha publications. For instance, they wrote for *Deutsche Zeitung in Kroatien*, for the Ustasha paper *Spremnost* ('Readiness'), for the journal *Za dom* ('For the Home'), for *Hrvatski narod* ('The Croatian nation') and *Hrvatski vojnik* ('The Croatian Soldier').

In addition to the beauty of the camp itself, Herman Pröbst was delighted by the work and good order there, as by the various products which the inmates made. And he said:

They showed us high boots, buckled straps, various leather and metal objects, bricks and tiles. A communist fitted red-hot links into a chain at remarkable speed. In one workshop for fine electrical mechanisms, delicate objects were made. In the brickworks a Jew wearing an enviably nice, fur-lined coat, gave a speech about his kilns… There was also a ceramics section, where some artists…

That is the article that was carried at the beginning of 1942 by the Ustasha paper *Spremnost* ('Readiness'), under the title 'Jasenovac is neither a health resort nor a torture chamber' and which is nowadays quoted by some who wish to maintain the continuity of Fascist, Ustasha propaganda. And now, after some fifty or so years, while some people (those who had failed then) endeavour to clear their name, ask forgiveness, confess their errors (these include both the Catholic Church and the International Red Cross), others howl the same old dead refrain, making history their serving girl.

Yes, since as early as February 1942, the Ustasha guard, like the Wehrmacht, organised exhibitions about life in the camps. In the NDH, the National State of Croatia, just as in the Third Reich, films about the camp idyll of fascist Croatia were shown in special, closed screenings. It's not an impossible idea that in those NDH camps the inmates really did rehearse and perform the lively operetta 'Little Floramye' just as the children in Terezin performed 'Brundibar'. Barka Antić recalls:

In the first transport from Stara Gradiška to Lepoglava, there were 450–500 prisoners. We sang 'Set off now through life with a song' for which the governor Ljuba Miloš punished us by denying us food for three days.

It is also plausible when people maintain that the camp inmates of the NDH participated in cultural events, singing and acting. Because that was done by inmates in all the prison camps of the world, always. Blinded, in their primordial dream, in a trance, the Ustasha supporters simply 'forgot' to mention what almost always followed those camp operettas and other productions.

Besides, the Nazis even ordered: 'Lied!' (Song!) and 'Singen' (Sing!) and round the necks of those who tried to escape and were caught, they hung a placard with the inscription: 'Hura, hura, ich bin wieder da!' ('Hurrah, hurrah, I have come back!') There is no reason to doubt that it was different in the NDH camps.

Hermine Braunsteiner was called 'The Mare of Majdanek'. She wore high polished boots. She was known for the kick she delivered, with the crack of a whip to the hungry camp inmates at Ravensbruck. She had a way with children. Before she took them to their death, she offered them sweets. If children annoyed her, she shot them in the head. She was born in Vienna in 1919 and brought up in a strict Catholic family. She joined the SS in 1939; and then worked as a guard in concentration camps in Poland. In 1948, the Tribunal for War Crimes in Austria condemned Hermine Braunsteiner to three years in prison. She was released nine months later. Until 1957, she worked as a shop-assistant in small tourist towns in Austria, then she met her future husband, the American Russell Ryan and went with him to Halifax, Canada. From there they soon moved to the United States. Hermine Braunsteiner-Ryan lived calmly until 1968. Under pressure from the government and public opinion, she voluntarily renounced American citizenship. She was extradited to West Germany in 1973. With another sixteen accused, she was condemned of the murder of 'at least 1,181' camp inmates and participating in the murder of another 705 people. The sentence was passed in 1981, when Hermine was 61. She was sentenced to life imprisonment. If she is still alive, she is in prison in Düsseldorf.

Joseph Kisielatis was a tailor in a Nazi police battallion which, it is believed, sent 130,000 Jews, Gypsies and 'others' from Eastern

Europe to their deaths. In the Lithuanian town of Kaunas, that same battallion was also capable of shooting up to 9,200 people in a single day. At the end of the war, Kisielatis turned up in a camp for displaced and persecuted people. That camp was visited one day by a trade union delegation of Canadian tailors looking for workers for their country. Kisielatis satisfied their criteria. He lived in Canada for ten years, then for twenty-one years in the United States, then in Canada again. In this case as well, over the years a bit of dust was raised over the war record of Joseph Kisielatis, but he and his family endured all the journalistic hullabaloo, and every judicial intervention, stoically and silently. If he is still alive, it is presumed that he is in Montreal.

Alexander Laak, a fifty-year-old originally from Estonia, hanged himself in his garage in Winnipeg, Canada, a week after the Soviets had pronounced him a war criminal. Tass accused Canada of protecting the former governor of a concentration camp responsible for the death of more than three thousand people between 1942 and 1943.

This whole story is very long. The following people have also passed through Canada or lived there in relative peace: Albert Helmut Rauca[33] and Imre Finta[34]. Then Michael Pawlowski, Jacob Luitjens, Stephen Reistetter, Radisav Grujičić, 'Felix', Arthur Rudolph, Erichs

---

33 SS sergeant. In the nineteen-sixties, in West Germany, accused of collaboration in the murder of 10,500 people in October 1941 in Kaunas, Lithuania. The Germans sought his extradition - with no response from Canada. The Germans tried again in 1970, 1973 and finally 1982. Albert Helmut Rauca was arrested in his home in Toronto and sent to Frankfurt in 1983. He died before the beginning of the court case in the prison hospital.

34 Arrested in Canada in 1987. As a Nazi collaborator he was accused of participating in the forced deportation of more than 8,600 Jews from Hungary to Austria and Polish concentration camps. At his trial in 1989, the charge was dropped. The 'Finci Case' reached the Supreme Court in 1992 and in 1994 the Supreme Court concluded that in the framework of the existing Law about War Criminals, it was impossible to reach a verdict. The case was placed *ad acta*.

Tobiass, Joseph Nemsila. Not one Canadian was convicted. Those who were extradited and tried in Europe were either released or served a symbolic part of their sentence. (It is therefore unlikely that the former commander of the Jasenovac camp, Dinko Šakić, on his extradition from Argentina, will fare any worse.)

Why had I not set off to investigate the lives of war criminals from the time of the Independent State of Croatia (NDH)? *Because it's all the same old story. Ante Pavelić, the NDH 'Poglavnik',[35] was aware of his historical role. He knew full well that he was the leader of an extremist movement and state formation that came into being through the will of the Duce and Führer and not an 'Ustasha revolution'. Of course, people crowed and trumpeted the opposite, but it is hard to believe that this able political fox (executioner in his own chicken coop) believed what he said in public, praising, for example, the resurrection of the 'Croatian kingdom' (1941), and then banging on about his 'two-faced ally' (1943).... It often occurs to me that in fact Ante Pavelić had just one fixed idea. That idea can only be compared to Hitler's 'final solution'. That idea was not, of course, the liquidation of Gypsies and Jews. The first were a 'quantité negligeable' for the purity of the national composition of the National State of Croatia. The second were intimately connected with the Ustasha present and past: Josip Frank was a Jew, Pavelić's wife Mara had Jewish blood, the mother of Dido Kvaternik would have been obliged, according to her son's regulations, to wear a yellow badge but she preferred the Mirogoj cemetery, etc. Besides, a large number of Jews became Croats and considered themselves Croats. Pavelić's Jewish (Jasenovac) policy was a concession to Nazism and not part of the Ustasha strategy.[36]*

---

35 Leader or 'Führer'. {Translator's note}

36 One should not forget that of all the countries allied to Hitler's Reich, two deserve particular praise for their zeal in their solution of the Jewish question. They are Slovakia and (Kvaternik's) Croatia. In a 'small business annex' of the protocol signed on 20th January 1942 in the villa on the Wannsee lake,

Pavelić saw his mission as just one thing: to cleanse Serbs from the Croatian ethnic and historical space, that is the NDH, as it looked after September 1943, adding the regions of Istria and Međimurje (which Pavelić was never able to include in his state).... Pavelić saw his greatness and his vocation in freeing forever the Croats from their 'cancer wound' or 'the Serbian question', because after him Croatia would remain nationally 'pure' on all its 'state-legal' territory: "Future Croatian regimes (if mine were to fall) will have various problems, but they will no longer have the Serbian problem!"[37] I did not research further, because, all that Fascism, that nationalism, that xenophobia, all those right-wing groups, yesterday and today, are all nothing but a pile of shit. They always were and always will be.

Grossberlin, which is today in the Holocaust Museum in that same villa, it states: (I'm quoting from Slobodan Šnajder's 'Vila na jezeru Wann' ['The villa on the Wann lake'], *Novi list*, 25 April, 1995.) *Killing implies machinery, which, although more or less on the whole serviced by slave labour, still entails some costs. Thus Germany, as a country-recipient and, in the end, donor of services, emphasised its price list in relation to the country-supplier. According to this price list, Slovakia was charged between 300 and 500 Reichsmarks for each supplied Jew, and the French as much as 700 Reichsmarks. Friendly Germany, however, had some understanding of the problems of its ally Croatia, so the same services – receiving Jews, taking out their gold teeth, shaving their heads and cleansing them with Cyklon B, cost only 30 Reichsmarks. It's true, it was only 30 Reichsmarks, but it should be remembered that Croatia was the only country-supplier that complied with this obligation! ... A fleeting glance at the copious, three-volume memoirs of the Austrian Glaise von Horstenau, who ... was Hitler's plenipotentiary, a kind of parallel authority in a more or less occupying regime inside a typical satellite Fascist metastasis like the unfortunate NDH, makes one think that the Germans, at least in his words, accused Pavelić's executioners of an excess of zeal, particularly towards the 'rebellious Serbs'. As for the Jews, perhaps for a person who thinks and feels Croatian, and that at every moment means anti-Ustasha, and so it will be till Judgment Day, there is no sadder document than the protocol in the lovely villa on the Wannsee, Grossberlin.*

37 Stanko Lasić: *Krležologija, Miroslav Krleža i Nezavisna Država Hrvatska* (10.4.1941. – 8.5.1945.), Globus, Zagreb 1989, Volume 3, pp. 157-158.

III

From the balcony I see a small residential building. A young woman lives there who comes out onto her terrace from time to time and shouts: *I am God! God, can you hear me? I am God!* Sometimes she smears her face with a brown colour and ties a leather band over her forehead so she looks like an Indian, and then shouts again: *I am God!* There are days when she is very angry. Then she throws things onto the street: books, rubbish, clothes. There are days when she keeps changing her clothes: from evening dresses with gloves up to her elbows she slips into short trousers and summer sleeveless T-shirts, then she puts on a winter coat and sandals with nothing on underneath, then an elegant suit and high-heeled shoes, but no stockings. There are days when she goes to the nearby crossroads, cruises round the very straight corners of that crossroads, marking out with her footsteps huge imaginary rectangles. She often has a long cigarette holder in her mouth, with a lit cigarette in it and waves her arms, with her head thrown back, with every step she bends her knees and hops, as though doing gymnastics or as though she were preparing to fly.

Her windows are always lit. She has decorated the terrace balustrade with various different coloured mushrooms, little caps with zigzag edges, blue, yellow, green and pink. And those mushrooms glow. She has floral curtains. Everything about her place is brightly coloured and cheerful.

I watch that woman every day. I look into her windows even when she's not on the terrace, when she's not at the crossroads. As time goes by, I am ever less certain whether that woman is just an unknown neighbour from the other side of the street, or whether that woman is perhaps actually me. I know that my meeting with Konrad Koše and the confrontation with his past, with the past of his parents, was a quite ordinary occurrence, a quite possible phenomenon for many of my generation all over the world. What kind of small dramas and family historical pages open up in Germany, for instance? Or in Japan? Or South America and North America? The President of Croatia would like to mix the bones of the victims of Fascism with those of their executioners. The President of Croatia would like to reconcile, if not actually the victims and their executioners, then at least their offspring. How naïve! How senseless! The bones are already well mixed, all over the world. Not thinking, not knowing, not searching, not wishing to search, the offspring of both, the victims and the executioners, fall in love, make new children, and the grandfathers of those children (victims and executioners, those who are still alive), dandle their grandchildren on their knees with a sense of profound historical and personal defeat.

But for me that was too much. Becoming increasingly like the woman from the other side of the street I was becoming increasingly bad for Konrad. Sara and I were again left alone.

IV

When she was still little and happy, Sara used to chatter ceaselessly in the morning. I remember myself getting up, always light and cheerful. And just as talkative.

Sara would chatter, I wouldn't listen to her. Getting up for me is now difficult, I'm morose and I wake slowly. My blood pressure is low.

Sara would talk, she talked very fast, in a voice too high and thin for my liking (in the afternoons Sara's voice was not at all chirpy), and from time to time she would check (it seemed to me always at regular intervals) whether I was listening to her sufficiently atten-tively, because Sara is sharp and always notices when my mind wanders. And every time she orders me, sternly:

Repeat what I just said!

Then I focus. The older I get, the more afraid of Sara I am because the older I get the older and bigger and stronger is my Sara.

From her biology lessons at school Sara brings home condoms and blows them up. We blow them up together. And with mild, very mild excitement, as though it was a matter of interesting but unfamiliar things to us adults, she tells me how they practise putting on the contraceptives with a model of a penis made from wood the colour of ivory. During the class, Donald, her contemporary, demonstrated letting superfluous air out of the condom, so as to make space for the sperm. No one had ever taught me that: how to prepare a condom, how to get it ready for use. In my day they were slipped on secretly, under the sheets.

There were deflated condoms all over the apartment.

In our time Ivana and I used to fill them with water and throw them from the apartment they owned on the sixth floor. That was a very long time ago, when privately owned apartments were rare, and the two of us already students and theoretically sexually almost perfectly well versed, but physically and mentally alarmingly innocent. The explosion of the inflated condoms was miraculously loud, like a kind of mocking laugh; the retired widows from the building opposite, leaning on their windows, with their flowering perlagoniums, shook their heads, shocked and disapproving. (All the windows of the grey-haired, retired and toothless widows looked the same, just as the retired widows themselves opposite Ivana's apartment all looked similar.) At that time no one talked about AIDS. Ivana collected the condoms secretly, because her mother was a strict history teacher in the strictest secondary school in the city. Ivana played at music school concerts and had little Chanel-type suits made by the most expensive seamstress. Her hands were bluish-red, often moist, which were a problem when she was playing (her fingers would slide disobediently and unpredictably over the keys), so she didn't take a music degree at the Academy, but studied Law. Whenever she answered questions at school (especially in history), sweat would drip off her hands, and also when she met with a boy. That sorted itself out later when Bojana was born.[38]

---

38 In 1997, it was six years since Sara and I had left Belgrade. For a good three years before our departure, I spent evening after evening at Ivana's in discussions about the political situation in former Yugoslavia. Then, after those discussions, we would go to some anti-war meeting, or demonstration of the like-minded, lighting candles for peace. Between 1989 and 1991 our lives were governed by politics. Absolutely. When we moved to Rijeka, to start with Ivana sent letters which I answered immediately. Then, silence. I know that her son went to Brazil to avoid being drafted into Milošević's military and paramilitary formations. I know that she had put on weight, that she had four cats and that she was on her own. Telephone connections between Croatia and Serbia were still broken so, before our departure for Canada, I went by train from Rijeka to Ilirska Bistrica and from a miniature post office from where you could call exclusively Serbia and Bosnia, I dialled 753-229 and told Ivana that we were leaving. We didn't mention politics.

When Sara got tired of playing with condoms, she began expecting her period. We went to buy the fine small thin pads, which are plentiful in Canada, then we waited, but no sign of menstruation. Then, one night her period came, but Sara didn't realise that it had. Then we went to celebrate with Prince's doughnuts bought at a Danish cake shop where everything smelled of Christmas.

I've got 'struation too, and an operation

Two-year-old Sara was standing in the middle of the room, with her panties down and a whole roll of toilet paper between her legs, and

Help, pease, mama's bathing, and she's got 'struation, shouts three-year-old Sara to the alarmed tourists on the beach.

We're going to buy panties, no more nappies, calls little Sara to passers-by and on the way makes up songs and sings:

to be born a butterfly and see the soul inside is what I want…

It passed too quickly.

Then there was a very important technical examination in the first year of primary school,

you have to bring your health card and be bathed and washed behind the ears because that's the most important thing for technical examinations

then on 29 November 1989[39], a formal reception in the organisation of little pioneers with starched red scarves round their necks. (At the Army Centre people still sang so-called songs of battle and rebuilding – *raise our foreheads high… , we will regain the whole land… may work live on and on.*) Photographers immortalised it at ten German Marks a photo.

When I proposed at parents' meetings that on that day and on future twenty-ninth of Novembers the children should be taken on

---

39 'Republic Day' in Tito's Yugoslavia, a public holiday. {Translator's note}

outings, into the countryside, instead of into centres with soldiers, I was thrown off the parents' committee. I spoke too soon, and unnecessarily, because less than two years after *little pioneers you are a true army, with each day you'll grow like the green grass,* they began one, two, to be mown down by shells and bombs and everything fell apart, the whole theatre went up in smoke. I took Sara to Rome on that 29th November 1989, because I still had money then and three free days, and 'Yugotours' offered attractive, reasonable packages.

You're traumatising the child, said those closest to me. *She should remember Republic Day all her life, you're depriving her of memories,* as though Rome isn't remembered one's whole life, you fools. Sara never mentioned Pioneers' Day again. And the photograph got lost somewhere, while Rome continues to stand where it has for centuries. So have the images of Rome in our memories: the cats on Campo dei Fiori, which Sara wanted to take (we always had problems with cats) into a hotel on the Campo dei Fiori (does every town have a Flower Square?), where public executions were once carried out, while today everything is colourful, clean and very picturesque. The ice-cream that ran in white rivulets down Sara's forearm as far as her armpit in Via delle Vacche, and Sara smelled of milk as when she was very, very small, and I didn't dream that a mere three years later I would regularly cross what is now my favourite, miniature Dairy Square in Rijeka, in order to conjure up images of that happy Roman excursion. Wishes, secret little prayers spoken almost furtively and sheepishly to oneself, under cover of the cascading fountains in the parks of the Villa d'Este, both of us with hands wet from the attempt to catch those wishes, those little dreams, but they fled because they were ordinary little drops of water.

It passed too quickly.

When I was taken to hospital, I just had time to give Sara a few phone numbers in Rijeka, Rovinj and Zagreb, to tell her where our passports were and who was looking after the money for our return journey. Then I spent a week grappling with an ugly woman who grabbed my hair in her hand as she breathed down my neck, and shouting 'Go away!' to her! I was tired and Sara was still small.

In Toronto Sara spoke English in her sleep, *I'm so happy, going to China Town to buy a turtle, going swimming, going to the school dance when I feed my cat,* while I look down on her, the windows are open, a quiet Canadian summer night, no longer at all threatening, creeps over the walls, as though cosying up to them. I look down on Sara, who smiles in her sleep

she looks like my mother, she looks terribly like my mother, if I took her in my arms would it be the same, my mother is not so small and blond and soft and fragrant, my mother's cheeks are grey with cobalt radiation, all my mother's skin is grey, thin, my mother's skin is so thin, with that scar from a burn on her right calf from the time when at thirteen she used to sing songs in French and the rag doll for which my grandfather –

I never saw that grandfather the wig-maker from Zagorje –

for which my grandfather the wig-maker and Viennese communist made real hair

but the rag doll caught fire and burned up in my thirteen-year-old mother's arms

Sara is thirteen and has beautiful blond hair

my mother's hair fell out from cytostatic treatment, there were no longer curls, her hair burned, my mother is a handful of ash, a handful of ash in a tin urn in a grave under the protection of the state (Serbia), where Paško Vučetić from Split, his wife Marija, the painter and sculptor Paško Vučetić

we didn't manage to make a list of his works in the Belgrade City Museum, Granny Ana kept going on about it, go to the museum, go on, I wrote a diary about a sailor from Kotor, in the grave above which stands Paško's sculpture 'Boy from Čukur pump', holding some kind of broken jug, a broken jug,

the 'B' variant, or maybe 'C', Paško from Split didn't have any children

I whisper the little poems that Sara finished that morning and called *Wheat, A Collection of Poems*, with no reference to wheat anywhere.

> *Today death was in my pocket,*
> *it hid in my shadow,*
> *then it slid into my hair,*
> *today death was in me.*

> > *My sea is only mine.*
> > *Little,*
> > *hidden in my pocket, it talks, wriggles*
> > *and rustles.*
> > *On paper*
> > *it makes a picture in the shadow.*
> > *My little sea*
> > *lives*
> > *sings*
> > *and*
> > *spreads its scent*
> > *within me.*

Pockets are very important for Sara.

Toronto is gradually imploding. I wonder whether others notice it and what they think about it. I'm glad about its implosion. It means that Toronto is getting closer to some other towns, far from me now, and with that closeness my hope grows that I will be able to live here.

Mice have appeared in the tunnels of the underground. You see them at every station. For the time being, they are little mice, less than five centimetres long, small and very quick.

At first, they ran along the tracks, *it's good they're quick, they won't get squashed, look, they're drinking water from the polluted puddles* then they got braver and moved onto the platforms. They whirl around between the passengers' feet. There are most at night, when there aren't crowds and the trains are less frequent.

In the streets there are more and more young people at traffic lights who clean car windows for five cents. That didn't happen earlier, that certainly didn't happen at the time of the sudden blossoming of the state of Canada.

One morning I heard the noise of the trucks that empty the rubbish skips. Before that din would have been unimaginable, although well known to me, because in Rijeka I would wait for midnight (they always came at midnight directly under our windows) for the racket to pass before I went to bed.

Then I noticed broken shutters on some skyscrapers. Just as broken as in my grandmother Ana's neglected uncomfortable apartment in Zagreb, in the distant nineteen-sixties. Toronto was growing closer, more homely.

Maybe I could have found some kind of work in Toronto. Some small job like the one Zdravka found in Mr Goldfarb's telemarketing firm. Thirty-seven residents of the building at 187 Hardy Street work there. Twenty-five of them are from former Yugoslavia. Mr Goldfarb sells photocopiers, and Zdravka is a French teacher so she can telephone bilingually. Mr Goldfarb pays the minimum hourly rate of $7,80, decreed by law. Their cubicles are small, the windows closed, so that the noise from the street doesn't disturb conversations with potential customers, and the hours flexible – from 9am to 10pm. The questionnaires are very long, with some thirty questions; some of those questioned get irritated straight away and hang up, some are hooked and order a photocopier, sometimes even two, then Goldfarb is happy. Zdravka is increasingly tired, she reads less and less and goes increasingly often to garage sales where she buys heaps of second-hand good quality clothes, because she circulates round the Jewish quarters. Then she gives it all away (she gave me a new grey felt hat), because she doesn't have the space for it. Otherwise, Zdravka is very well-read. And she's clever, only there's no one here to see it. Goldfarb doesn't give a damn.

I made a few documentary programmes for the National Radio, but it wasn't possible to live on that. In six months, the state radio fired 2,400 employees all over the country. In front of the state radio building in Toronto, on an intensely green grassy expanse there's a group sculpture made of bronze: a flock of sheep (or perhaps lambs?) seemingly grazing. Whenever I go there, I spend a long time looking at those sheep in front of the state radio station in Toronto, completely entranced. Whenever I have a job in that state radio station (but that's increasingly rare), I arrive early and go to the little café and observe and listen to its productive labour force. At the beginning of every new working day, it, that labour force, relates its intimate life, shares its fears and joys; it's compact, it's a firm, homogeneous body.

I signed up for social support.

In the social welfare offices in Canada, you are assigned advisers as in the State Office for Immigrants. In the social welfare offices, however, those advisers have numbers instead of names. I was allocated adviser number 91. 91 informed me in writing on what day and at what I time I had to go for my first, informative, conversation. The local welfare office is housed in an attractive new building. It stands out a bit, because it is surrounded by large wooden houses, very dilapidated, oozing poverty. There's also a children's nursery in that building so that passers-by don't need to know who is going for assistance and who to collect a child. The area is problematic. It is inhabited largely by marginal citizens: prostitutes, transvestites, drug-addicts and alcoholics. Many women and men have tattoos on every visible part of them (face, neck, ankles, down their calves) and wear silver rings in their pierced lips, tongue, nostrils, eyebrows (the ones all around the ear have become trivial). The Office has a long corridor with a lot of blue doors, and behind the doors are small, unbelievably small cubicles (this seems to be a land of cubicles), each one divided vertically by a thick pane of glass with a narrow slit in the middle, so that the adviser and client can see and hear each other, but heaven forbid that they should touch. On each side of the glass there is a chair covered in white plastic. The walls are also white, everything is very white, almost dreamlike. Horizontally, at waist level, the space is cut through by a woodchip board (plastic-coated) – before each new interview, such plastic-coated surfaces can be easily wiped down with a disinfectant smelling of pine needles – on which the advisers spread printed sheets with the legal regulations, confidential information, government powers, the clients' obligations and his or her final signature. All of that passes through that narrow slit in the dividing wall of thick glass.

In Rijeka, Marieta didn't have any kind of number. Marieta had her name on the door. In her little office, with a view of ochre-coloured Austro-Hungarian buildings, surrounded by ancient pine trees, Marieta had a low coffee table from the nineteen-fifties, wooden, of course, and on either side of that little table there was a huge armchair, covered in cracked dark-green leather. Her desk was covered in 'cases', but when I first went to see her, she immediately abandoned her desk and sat down in the wide armchair opposite me. I took freshly bought peaches, cold and juicy, out of a carrier bag (I didn't know where to put myself from shame; but such shame later vanishes), we both ate and sucked and wiped our sticky chins with our forearms and so got to know each other. Having found a loophole in the law, Marieta gave me a one-off payment, *until the case is resolved, and that can take up to a month,* that's what she said. *I know it's only a little, but I can't give you any more than that,* she also said. Then I said: *Come and have some cakes with us; Sara and I haven't eaten decent cakes in the garden of a decent cake shop since our distant trip to Rome.* So, thanks to that little temporary support from the Republic of Croatia, Marieta, her then seven-year-old Eva and I and my then nine-year-old Sara went to the famous 'Simona' cake shop, right next to Mliječni trg (Dairy Square) and gorged ourselves on cakes with lots of custard and cream, while a breeze wafted softly from the sea. Later, in the course of our three-year stay in Rijeka, Marieta and I would often talk on the phone in the evening, once the rubbish trucks had long gone, and we would sometimes go to the cinema or theatre together and give each other little presents.

Not the slightest part of this, I realised, could ever be achieved with number 91.

Tia Rejdan (in English that's the way my name in this story, Tea Radan, is pronounced), *door 11!* came over the loudspeaker.

Filling in the form went smoothly, routinely and politely, until we got to Sara:

Father's name asks 91, without raising her head.

She has no father.

A child must have a father, we have to fill in that heading.

On her birth certificate, instead of a father's name there's a cross.

We can't use crosses, says 91 decisively. *Those are our instructions. Write: father unknown.*

Not possible. We have a search service that will find the father. We have to know whether she receives any financial help from her father.

She doesn't, I say. *Her father doesn't exist.*

I felt my heart beating faster. In fact, I was terrified, as I don't like detective or bugging or any of the other secret services I got to know in the time of my father's political work. I think, I think with great concentration, and I don't know what to do.

Let's go on, says 91 indulgently. *We'll come back to the name later. Eye colour?*

Eye colour? He's got no eyes.

Is he blind?

Could be. He doesn't exist.

Height? Weight? Address? 91 is impatient again. *I'm still thinking. You must cooperate. Your file will go to number 53. I'm just an intermediary. Number 53 is your permanent adviser and you are obliged to inform her regularly about the details and possible changes in your life, particularly changes in connection with the child's father? Hair colour.*

Hair colour? He's got no hair, I say.

Place of residence? 91 goes back to the beginning.

A palace! It's a palace, I exclaim with relief. (But a name, but a name, what do I do about the name?! She's going to ask again.)

But she didn't. The name didn't come till the end.

Height?

1 metre 60.

What's that in feet, we use feet here.

Little.

So, he's a small man. Small.

I felt a stifled delight, a fine tickling delight working from my stomach towards my throat. A small bald man, of not yet clear outline, was mysteriously surfacing in front of me.

Weight? 91 continued officially. *A hundred and three.*

A hundred and three what?

Kilograms.

What's that in pounds? We use pounds here.

230.

So, a heavy man, 91 went on indifferently and made a note. *Name?*

Croaticus Magnus! I brought up.

Spell that for me, we spell everything here, letter by letter, 91 commanded politely, but sternly.

I spelled it out, letter by letter. Croaticus Magnus.

Good, mumbled 91. Then, glad that she had somehow done her job, she added in an almost friendly tone: *You see that it wasn't terrible or difficult. You see that the child has a father.*

Yes, I agreed.

Just one small thing more: *how long did your relationship last??!*

91 really wanted to help. In an almost conspiratorial tone she suggested: *Shall we put: a brief encounter?*

Yes, I was delighted. *That sounds good and filmic.*

As a gesture of some small gratitude for her moral support in the course of the informative conversation that had just ended, I wanted to offer 91 my hand, but I was only able to poke my index finger through the narrow slit in the thick glass, so I wiggled it by way of greeting. 91 wiggled her own index finger in response.

It was a sunny day. I decided to go home on foot, which meant that I was in for two hours of brisk, steady walking. But I planned to break the walk with some food shopping, in a shop where they often had reductions. And in it, that mammoth supermarket, I'd buy a two-litre jar of mayonnaise and a tub of ice-cream, because it's soothing.

At home Sara was waiting for me, Sara is always waiting for me at home, and when Sara goes to a school dance, a netball match or to a friend's, I have my computer. My computer and I represent the Canadian labour force. The two of us are integrated. We travel the world together. We go to libraries together, we look at what's in them, we choose, then I sometimes hurry to take that home. My computer and I correspond with everyone dear to us. Should we need some special information, we contact unknown people or firms. That, the fact that my computer and I cannot see what the people with whom we are talking are wearing, what their hair is like, what their teeth are like, their smile, whether their voices are deep or shrill, how they smell, how they shake hands, how they walk, the fact that we cannot touch anyone – so what? There are worse things. Wars, for example.

I also had a forebear on my father's side about whom I know a little. He was my father's mother's father.

He lived in that village house in which later his son-in-law, my grandfather (the one who wrote the letter to Tito) was left alone and in whose garden he cultivated strawberries and grapes, not for his grandchildren (my brother, sister and me), but for his sons and to sell. In the garden of that house in the heart of Istria there is still a stone well with the initials of my great-grandfather P.U. engraved in a kind of family coat of arms. Whether that means that my ancestors were village landowners, I don't know, although the thought of such a possibility is amusing.

In that house, during the war, illegal meetings of Istrian anti-fascists were held and confidential documents and an old camera (which I have) were hidden in the walls. After the war, Party and State authorities affixed two marble plaques as a memento of the heroic war days. Then, in the course of the new war and independent Republic of Croatia, those plaques were smashed with hammers, annihilated. The memorials were cancelled, there were no more marble plaques on my ancestor P.U.'s house, a blessed oblivion reigned. The house had been bought before the collapse of socialist Yugoslavia by some people from Leskovac, Serbia, who chopped down the vines, killed the bees, dug up the strawberries, but never guessed what was hidden behind its attic walls. Then, in 1992, my father sold the last part of the family property, a dilapidated house in Rovinj, no longer now for idealistic reasons, but so that he would have something to eat, because Yugoslavia had fallen apart and his pension had remained in Belgrade.[40]

---

40 The business with my father's pension was later sorted so that today it is worth less than two hundred and fifty Euros a month.

In 1943, the Fascists issued a warrant for the arrest of my father and his brother. At that time my father and his brother were organising an uprising in Istria and were hiding in the Istrian forests. My grandmother, their mother and the daughter of my ancestor P.U., died in terrible pain from some then unidentified disease. The Fascists hoped that the Radan brothers would come, at least secretly, to visit their mother and, in the worst case, should she die, to her funeral, so they surrounded the house and placed well-armed guards all around it. My grandfather (the one who wrote the letter to Tito) was already drinking castor oil in an Italian prison. My great-grandmother was dead, so old P.U. was left to care for their sick daughter. That sick daughter, my grandmother, died, her sons didn't come, my great-grandfather buried her and moved into the attic. There he made little balls of his own excrement, one could say – marbles or even sheep's droppings. You could never say, however, that they were real marbles. Marbles have that brightly coloured eye in the centre, which is unbreakable. It would be more accurate to say droppings, although those are shat by goats or sheep and not people. There, in his attic, in 1944, my great-grandfather played solo games of miniature bowls with his own excrement. (Maybe that's why I love marbles; maybe it was imprinted in my genetic code.) There, in that attic, my great-grandfather and village landowner P.U. left his testament, writing his credo made from his own excrement and leaving it as a legacy to me.

Some relatives had wanted to marry off the grandfather who wrote a letter to Tito, my father's father, to my grandmother Ana. That way they envisaged that the family would be together, close and compact. It didn't work out because my grandmother Ana refused. Had she agreed, I would not have had to roam all over Croatia, from Zagorje, Split and Zagreb, to Karojba and Istria as a whole. All my relatives would have been here. As it is, I'm collecting their shit and my own (and the occasional marble), and piling it all up like a hamster in little hiding places, for my old age. Then I'll take it out and look at it.

Otherwise, writers (male and female) are the greatest gossip-mongers there are. They keep looking for something to make into some kind of pie. They discover, say, that there are no rivers in Denmark, they connect that with Hamlet and serve it up to their readers. They find that Canada, say, doesn't have a single kiosk but its scholarly literature about kiosks is abundant and serious, so they toss that into a story. That's what I do too. Like that young woman in my neighbourhood, the one with the multi-coloured illuminated mushrooms on her balcony who shouts *God, can you hear me?* Who often alters her appearance and voice, who dances at busy Canadian crossroads – like her, I too play.

HITLER LIKED QUAIL
AND FATHER CHRISTMAS
ABANDONS BOSNIA

Sikhs are the only people who walk around proudly in turbans and who have a lot of uncut hair because their faith doesn't allow them to remove or cut their own hair. They say that their faith is very progressive, it was far ahead of its time when it came into being five hundred years ago. They say that this faith of theirs is followed by twenty million people all over the world. Sikhism preaches devotion to God, equality among people, an honourable life and some other things, and it rejects prejudice and unfounded rituals. What constitutes an honourable life, according to the Sikhs' belief, and which rituals are unfounded, is not described in my little handbook, because it is assumed that everyone knows. Sikhism respects ten Gurus, and all ten are embodied in the currently living guru who is called Sri Guru Grant Sahib.

All this and a few other things about Sikhs, I learned only after my meeting, eye to eye, face to face, with a real devoted living Sikh.

The Christmas and New Year holidays were approaching. Toronto is a city with a lot of electricity and an unbelievable number of light bulbs of all sizes. The bare trees, for the most part dwarf, planted all along the broad avenues in the centre of the city, are decorated with small white berry-like lights, so it looks as though the trees are snowing, crisply, flakily, softly. The skyscrapers gleam under illuminations of imposing weight and size, that doesn't look so cheerful. There are many shops, a very great many and during the holidays they are festive and full of everything. Sara lost a trainer at school.

The Sikh faith rests on five symbols, on the famous five 'ks', that every devout (male) Sikh, bears until his death, having taken a pledge. These are: kesh (long hair), kanga (comb), kaccha (cotton underwear), kara (steel bracelet) and kharpan (sword). Listed like this, these five 'ks' seem harmless, but when they are seen together, on a real life Sikh walking in his house – barefoot, because Sikhs like to go barefoot – then, especially in winter, especially in some silent out-of-the way place, buried under heaps of banked snow at two in the morning and right outside the city of Toronto, then these 'ks' and that huge, bearded strapping Sikh can look quite intimidating.

We didn't know what to do with Sara's other trainer, because she does have two feet. Nevertheless, the remaining shoe stayed with us because it was a new Reebok of fine calf skin and it was worth, at least, fifty dollars. Otherwise, there are all kinds of trainers here, that is there are also cheap ones, but no one sells just one. It wouldn't bother Sara particularly to wear two different ones because she once did that in the fifth or sixth class of primary school – she wouldn't even have known that she had put on two different shoes as no one in the entire school mentioned it. Her feet are smaller than mine, but just as narrow, so if I can't actually wear her shoes, I can at least slip my feet into them.

Sikhs pray a lot. They open their holy book, Grant, three times a day, and read and recite prayers from it. Sikhs who go out to work have them recorded on a magnetic tape, those randomly selected prayers, they can't read them but they can listen, follow them and mumble. If they work outside a building, they pray with the help of a Walkman.

A good Sikh must resist sins. In that way, a good Sikh will earn God's mercy and become immortal. There are five mortal sins, the Sikhs believe: lust, anger, greed, attachment and selfishness. One can only truly love God when one ceases to love oneself. The Sikh faith proscribes idolatry of every kind, the consumption of alcoholic beverages and does not acknowledge castes. For the most part, all faiths sound fine and just, it's really fascinating.

But in the nineteen-eighties in India a nationalist and fairly militant party emerged among the Sikhs, whose aim was greater autonomy for their region of Punjab. There were demonstrations and sharp conflicts between Sikhs and Hindus, the government took measures – sending fifty thousand soldiers against the Sikhs and putting the Punjab under their control.[41]

At the end of the nineteen-nineties in Sarajevo there was a campaign against *Djed Mraz* (Grandfather Frost), that is against *Djed Božićnjak* (Grandfather Christmas). The campaign acquired somewhat greater and more militant dimensions than the campaign

---

41 Just after my adventure with the Sikhs came to an end and only after I had decided to write these few pages about this adventure, Canadian state television, CBC, began a three-day report about tensions that had broken out in Toronto between groups of militant, orthodox Sikhs and more moderate ones. The conflict took place outside one of their temples and was so violent that all the participants took out the knives and swords they kept hidden under their robes. The 'softer' group tried to bring their tables and chairs into the social rooms of the temple and along with them also cutlery, while the 'harder' element energetically opposed this. The hard group maintained that Sikhs ought to sit on the floor and eat with their fingers, regardless of the fact that they were living in a culture that was quite different from their own Sikh culture. There were casualties. People were wounded, with cuts to their faces and bodies, while the observers, non-Sikhs, followed it all in astonishment.

carried out in Croatia five years earlier, when it was decreed that the 'Serbo-communist' Grandfather Frost ought to be rechristened (transformed) into the Croato-Christian Grandfather Christmas. Representatives of the UN in Sarajevo reported that the campaign had already resulted in several incidents. The UN spokesman Aleksandar Ivanko announced that the editor of the independent radio station ISV had been badly beaten up because his radio station 'supported Grandfather Frost'. Ivanko stressed that attitudes to Grandfather Frost had suddenly become a political question: *Grandfather Frost is on his deathbed,* said Ivanko. *You can't find a single picture of him in the city any longer. Activists and supporters of the Party of Democratic Action are going round primary schools and urging them 'not to allow Grandfather Frost to bring the children presents'.* That all happened before new year 1997, three or four years before the beginning of the new millennium. The local police refused to write a report about the attack on the journalist from Radio ISV although the UN demanded that the perpetrators be revealed. The office of the High Representative of the international community in Bosnia, Carl Bildt, and the OSCE also condemned the attack. In an open letter to the public, the President of the Presidency of Bosnia and Herzegovina, Alija Izetbegović, described Christmas as an 'immoral festival', judging that *Grandfather Frost was not part of the culture of Bosnia and Herzegovina, but 'imposed from outside'. Grandfather Frost (Father Christmas) is one of the rare things that unites people, brings them closer, which is just why he is exposed to the attacks of extremists,* believes Ivanko.

The Sikhs don't have a Grandfather Frost-Father Christmas either. Their faith forbids the 'unification of people'.

Sara is a modest child, but she is a child. Here people buy a lot. What they buy doesn't matter. They buy even what they already have, especially if it's in a sale. Two words here are very frequent: saving and sale. *Buy three pairs of panties – get one free! Buy a dozen cakes, the thirteenth is free!* The savings are on the whole small, especially in relation to the advertisements, which are big and loud. That's how people live here. Buying is a cult. Now Sara has been infected and she constantly needs something, something that has to be bought.

In a cake-shop I arranged doughnuts in little floral cardboard boxes. Vlatko found that job for me through his connections. It smelled good there but it didn't last long. For two whole days I arranged doughnuts in the back kitchen and earned about a hundred dollars. We spent that immediately on basic supplies because our fridge was empty. The holidays were very close. I spent three days taking advertisements round houses. Mladen found that job for me through his connections. I put some of the advertisements in little mailboxes, some under the doors. I lost three kilos because I had to walk a lot and it was very cold outside. There's a biting wind in Toronto, compared to which our north wind is trivial. When that wind blows, a temperature of minus ten Fahrenheit immediately falls to minus twenty-five. When it rains and a person is distributing advertisements, they usually get drenched because it's impossible to carry both the advertisements and an umbrella at the same time, because he (or she) needs both hands just for the leaflets. Leaflets require the whole person. I distributed them by night, after confirming with Sara the structure of an atom, the geographical breadth and length of the main cities round about, after correcting the spelling mistakes in her essay about Golding's *The Lord of the Flies* and, for my own sake, like someone absolutely obsessed, listening ten times to Dina Vierny singing ballads about Stalin's Gulags. The words of those ballads were written by prisoners. Those prisoners are now on the whole dead, so why do their verses concern me so much? I ask everyone whether they know about Dina Vierny and her ballads. No one does. I used to listen to them long ago, when they belonged to the Soviet underground and were taken secretly out of the country. Nowadays Dina Vierny's ballads are widely sold, they are recorded on CDs but they aren't relevant anymore; few people buy them because few people know about them. Especially here, in Canada. Why should people in Canada be concerned about some remote Dina Vierny and the ballads of Soviet prisoners. Who's heard of Kolyma, or Vorkuta?[42]

42 *If space in history books were allotted in proportion to human suffering, then Vorkuta would warrant one of the longest chapters. From 1932 until 1957, this mining town on the Pechora river, in Russia's Arctic, stood at the centre of Europe's most extensive complex of concentration camps. In Stalin's 'Gulag Archipelago', the "vorkutlag" ranked second only to Kolyma in north-eastern Siberia … At the time of the "zek" rebellion in 1953, Vorkuta held some 300,000 souls. Over the years more human beings perished there than in Auschwitz; and they died slowly, in despair. But few history books remember them. There are many eye-witness reports from Vorkuta, several of them published in English; but few people have read them. There is even a detailed guidebook to over 2000 'facilities' of the Soviet Gulag written by a Jewish survivor in the 1970s. His account was barely noticed … At the height of the Glasnost era, local people started digging in the Kuropaty Forest near Minsk in Belarus. They knew that it sheltered the remains of men, women and children killed during the Great Terror fifty years before. They uncovered several circular pits, each containing a mass grave for c. 3,000 bodies. They could see that scores, if not hundreds, more such pits lay under the pines. But in 1991 they were ordered to stop. They planted a cross by the roadside, and left the secrets of the forest intact. In 1989 the Russian 'Memorial' organization, which devotes itself to discovering the truth about Stalinist times, unearthed a pit at Chelyabinsk in the Urals, dating from the 1930s. It contained 80,000 skeletons. Bullet holes in skulls told an unambiguous story. They were not victims who had been worked to death in the Gulag. 'People were taken out of their flats,' said the local photographer, 'and shot with their children at this place.'[…] No medieval institution has attracted greater opprobrium from later ages than the Holy Inquisition. To many modern commentators, the ferocity aroused during the pursuit of heretics, Jews or witches is often incomprehensible […] Yet a little reflection suggests that the phenomenon is not exclusively medieval [...] Comparisons have been made between the Inquisition [… and] the treatment of dissidents to the Soviet regime, who in the 1980s were still regularly consigned to psychiatric clinics, diagnosed as 'schizophrenic' and forcibly*

That was all the distant past. Those who remember, those who know and are here don't want to remember. They can't even remember because they are very old. For example Ljuba, a Polish Jewish woman transported in 1939 from Warsaw to Karaganda. I've no idea why I took to the songs of Dina Vierny. They have no connection whatever with my life. Those political ballads from Ljuba's day are a whole world away from mine. They are ballads of lost opportunities. They are dead ballads. For instance, one about Stalin:

Comrade Stalin, you are a learned man,
you are highly educated,
while I'm an ordinary Soviet prisoner
and my companion is a grey forest wolf.

Why I'm here, I really don't know,
but the prosecutor must have been right
because here I am in the Tarukhansk region
where you too were deported
in the days of the Emperor.

Here I am in the Tarukhansk region
where the guards are rough and stupid
which of course I understand
as part of the class struggle.

With a Party cap on your head
I see you at a parade

---

disabled with drugs […] The Catholic Prince-Bishop of Bamberg, Johan Georg II Fuchs von Dornheim, possessed a purpose-built witch-house, complete with torture-chamber adorned with biblical texts. In his ten-year reign (1623-33) he is said to have burned 600 witches. […] And there is an important comparative aspect: the collective hysteria and false denumciations of witch-hunting have much in common with the phenomena of Jew-baiting and of the Communist purges. Norman Davies, *Europe, A History,* Oxford University Press, London, 1996, pp. 454, 566, 567, 963.

while we chop wood and, as in the past,
Stalinist splinters scatter in all directions.

Despite the snow,
despite the clouds of mosquitoes,
we spend the whole day in the taiga,
because here your sparks fly
And thank you, comrade Stalin,
I warm myself at your fire.

Yesterday we buried two Marxists
and we didn't cover them with a red flag.
One was a left-winger,
and the other was condemned for no reason.

Live for a thousand years for us, comrade Stalin,
and however hard the days are for me here,
statistics will show that there is now more iron,
more steel, per head of the population.

Dina Vierny sings and I sit enchanted and am late in distributing the advertisements. I distributed them at night also in case anyone should happen to see me. When I had distributed three thousand, my little contract came to an end and I bought a small black leather hat. I bought Sara paints. I bought food and litter for the cat, two dozen eggs and a kilo of fresh cheese because I have reached an age when I need calcium. It was 22nd December, we still didn't have a Christmas tree, traditional salt cod was out of the question and we didn't have anything to put under that non-existent Christmas tree. Marina gave me a sour cabbage; I hate sour cabbage. There's a woman called Lily nearby who sells sour cabbage, but since I don't like talking to her, I don't go there. Then Esad phoned:

There's a job working for a Sikh, filling envelopes. Six dollars an hour.

Okay, I said, although six dollars an hour was two dollars less than the minimum wage guaranteed by law in Canada.

Esad whispered that to me while we were watching a production for Croatian immigrants called 'Christmas in Lonjica', devised by a Croato-Canadian hairdresser, very bleached[43] , otherwise from the town of Lonjica which no longer exists on the map. I didn't give a damn about Christmas in Lonjica; I kept thinking about salt cod and fritters with pine-nuts and grappa the way my aunt Ljube in Split used to make it. At that play, performed in a local school right outside Toronto sentimentally and clumsily by members of the Croatian immigrant community, mostly amateurs in acting and

---

43 One could say that the bleached Croatian-Canadian hairdresser, originally from Lonjica, was well established in Toronto. She had earned substantial capital inventing special hair dyes, a variant of titian-red, after which there were lots of similar titian-red-haired women all around. The middle-aged hairdresser possessed a villa with a dozen rooms some hundred kilometres outside Toronto, and in the middle room the central attraction was an open stove around which her guests gathered in winter. Who were her guests? Her guests were on the whole the more educated members of the Croatian immigrant community (and the occasional Canadian among them). The hairdresser from Lonjica invited into her splendid home engineers, architects, doctors, sociologists, composers – enthusiasts of the theatre who came together round the creator of the Croatian Christmas production about Croatian Christmas in Lonjica, and with the aid of her staff, permanent or borrowed for the occasion – mostly from the Philippines – she put on a 'stylish' gathering round a cheerful fire and colourful canapés. So the hairdresser from Lonjica, as the author of occasional populist dramatic texts with a flavour of the naïve and with an undoubted talent for portraying the authentic nature of a Croatian village through the perspective of the splendid dominant kitsch, in the cacophony of conversations of her educated guests, built her own image, a small 'elite' nest, her magic mirror, some hundred kilometres outside Toronto, where in winter there is a lot of snow and nothing else. And they, architects, stage designers, painters, engineers and doctors, visited her at the weekend, why not, it was pleasant and relaxing in that palace, in the peace of wild and untouched nature they exchanged ideas while the hairdresser from Lonjica planned dinner in the back kitchen with her staff. And everyone was happy. And everyone was satisfied. That was, presumably, that new class.

theatrical skills, they sold little dry cakes made in the kitchens of worthy Croatian housewives, sold cassettes of medleys of folk songs and dances, played tamburitzas, all so traditional and cheerful, but since I am not a traditional person, I found it hard to fit in.

On my way with Esad to the agreed night-time work for the Sikh (night-time because it was illegal), I saw for the first time since I had been in Canada mimosa in a flower shop. It's too cold here for mimosa but they were my late mother's favourite flower and my brother often bought them for her. The average Canadian (the majority) had no idea that mimosa was a flower. The average Canadian said at once that mimosa was an interesting drink, in fact a cocktail made with orangeade and champagne. On the same day, I learned that the Board of the Mimosa Festival in Herceg Novi had agreed the programme of the festival, which would run from 17th January to the 1st March 1997. In the announcement it said that it was not yet certain whether the caravan would go on tour outside Herceg Novi (where the caravan had been intended to go was not mentioned in the announcement), because the Foreign Minister of Montenegro, Janko Jeknić, otherwise a member of the Mimosa Festival Board, recommended that the Mimosa caravan should not go on tour, but visitors should come to Herceg Novi, as happened in all festival towns all over the world. If the Foreign Minister would make an effort to get Herceg Novi to export some mimosa to Canada, the average Canadian would get to know its tender, fragrant yellow flower and would not confuse it with an orange bubbly drink.[44] The mimosas I had seen in the Toronto

44 A month after writing this text, I read the following news item: **Janko Jeknić, Foreign Minister of Montenegro, dies** - Janko Jeknić, Foreign Minister of Montenegro lost his life in a car crash. The accident happened on the Podgorica-Nikšić motorway, reported the Republican Secretariat of Information of Montenegro officially. Unofficially it was learned that the car being driven by Jeknić collided with a broken-down bus parked by the roadside. Again

flower shop had come from southern Italy and cost more than orchids, because there are all kinds of orchids here, large and small, while there is no mimosa. Some things here are valued for their scarcity. Orchids are crossed in Canadian laboratories, so there are all kinds and sizes of them, but that's probably more difficult with mimosa since it grows on a tree.

The papers are full of advertisements for small household jobs, shady deals, which allegedly pay. They include reading books and stuffing envelopes.

To get to the black-market filling of envelopes in the house of a Sikh, one travelled by bus north to the last stop, on the periphery of the city. It was warm in the bus, while a snowstorm raged outside. The bus was almost empty because it was seven o'clock in the evening and people had got home from work and that was the time they had dinner. At the last bus stop there was an enormous shopping centre. At the eastern entrance immigrant workers, on the whole Bosnian, gathered, eager for the underground work, because it was carried out in a cellar. I learned that when Esad asked me:

Did you bring slippers?
Why slippers?

---

according to unofficial sources, the accident happened at about four in the morning on the section of road near the source of the Mareza river. It was officially announced that on the occasion of the tragic death of Minister Jeknić, a committee had been established for the funeral, headed by the President of Montenegro, Momir Bulatović. A memorial meeting would be held in the building of the Montenegrin Government and the funeral that same day in the Podgorica cemetery. The late Janko Jeknić was born in 1949 in Kotor. He was first elected Foreign Minister of Montenegro in 1995. He had graduated from the Economics Faculty in Podgorica, and his career biography stresses that he was Consul for Economic Affairs in the Yugoslav General Consulate in Milan and chief of the Republic's Protocol. The late Minister Jeknić had four children from two marriages. As may be seen from the report, there was no mention of mimosa anywhere.

Because you stay there a long time, until the envelopes for that day are filled, sometimes till four in the morning, sometimes five, and your feet freeze.

Why?

Because you take your shoes off.

Why?

Because that's what the Sikhs want.

I had imagined that I would be able to stay for as long as I liked, according to the principle 'so much music, so much money', but later I saw that, in the case of stuffing envelopes at the Sikhs that principle wouldn't work, because as soon as they had unloaded us, I realised that there was nothing anywhere around, no houses or dogs, let alone people or telephone booths and secondly, even if I had decided on secret flight from that snowed-up house, I would have had to do it in socks, because as soon as you enter the Sikhs' house they put your shoes away somewhere, probably just so that you don't run away. And walking in socks through snow at night would be stupid because I wasn't going so far as to risk my life, presumably.

How many envelopes are there in one lot? I asked Esad.

Between five and six thousand, he said.

I immediately broke out in a cold sweat but then, also at the same moment, I began to calculate, in the hope of cheering myself up: from seven in the evening until five in the morning – ten hours, times six (dollars), equals sixty, equals a pair of tennis shoes in a sale for Sara, equals a little cheerfulness under a decorated Christmas tree. Do you know what six thousand envelopes are? Do you have the slightest notion of what six thousand envelopes look like strewn over a table?

In the meeting place (there were four of us there), I saw Mirsada, an architect from Sarajevo, who had come to Toronto, with her son, two years earlier, on the same plane as Sara and me. I noticed Mirsada at once at the airport in Zurich where all of us who had arrived from various parts of the former Yugoslavia were stuffed, after waiting for six hours, into one single, enormous Canadian Boeing. Mirsada had floated through the Swiss airport shops in an open soft black coat of the latest design so as to show that under the coat she was wearing a very chic suit of grey suede. She had pitch black hair, cut like Mireille Mathieu or, for those who don't remember Mireille Mathieu – like Prince Valiant. She looked self-confident, a little irritated and, unlike the majority of us anxious future immigrants, at that Swiss airport Mirsada looked like a real international traveller, like a successful businesswoman. In the duty-free shop she bought a lot of different small extravagant things: anti-wrinkle cream, an 850 gram 'Toblerone', a watch for her son, a 'Dior' silk scarf and 'L'air du temps' scent, which I like too.

At the meeting point for labourers from the former Yugoslavia working illegally for the Sikhs, at the eastern entrance to the 'Fairview' shopping centre, where from above, from the ceiling, some kind of machine blows out warm air so waiting at minus twenty isn't so terrible, that's where I caught sight of Mirsada, the architect from Sarajevo. What I saw was in fact a pale, grey-haired woman wearing brown plastic shoes, shivering in a crumpled grey raincoat.

Where's that coat of yours? I ask.

So, you didn't find a job, Mirsada concluded.

How's your son? I asked her then. She shed a few tears, and said: *My son. My son has left school. He's loading boxes for a company. What about your husband, did your husband come?*

No, said Mirsada.

Is that the same bag you had at the airport? I'm surprised.

How come you remember? It was Mirsada's turn to be surprised. *It looks smaller.*

Did you bring slippers?

Here I was really unsettled. I wanted to go home straight away, I suddenly wanted to hug my beautiful, clever, good Sara, whom I'm always moaning at about something, whom I shout at when she loses a trainer, and who is secretly, at night, completing a large oil painting – for me, to go under the tree.

Then Zafir arrived at the meeting point in his shiny metallic blue van. Zafir used to run a café, a pub, or something in Bijeljina, Bosnia. In Toronto he became a personal, special friend of the Sikh to whom he had taken us to fill envelopes. The door of Zafir's metallic blue van doesn't open outwards but slides from left to right, quietly, very filmically. Zafir piled us in, all four of us, onto the back seats; on the front seat, next to him, sat his mobile telephone. Then, without turning round because he was just typing in a number, he asked:

Have you brought slippers?

No one said a word.

Then again: I'm asking you, Tea: *have you brought slippers?*

I started rummaging through my bag to give myself some time. I too have a large black bag, which I bought in Trieste for 160,000 lira before I left for Canada. As it's all I've got it does me for everything and, like Mirsada's, it's shabby. I dug around for a while, and then stopped. At the bottom, beside a necklace of Japanese pearls that Deneš Vajs (or perhaps Dana the Partisan) had given my mother in the late nineteen-sixties, and which I dragged around everywhere with me, in case of need (I calculated that they must be worth at least a hundred), and saw Sara's remaining trainer. There was a note in the trainer: Wake me when you get home.

I've got something… , I said.

Okay, Zafir replied in an official tone, and then in terrible English, really, really terrible English, he informed his personal, special friend the Sikh that we would soon be there.

When we arrived, just as I had feared, everyone took off their shoes and some quiet women in saris swirled around us and then vanished. With them, with those quiet, lovely, meek and gentle women in saris, went our coats and – all our shoes.

Zafir took us into the cellar. The others all knew their way around, only I was new. The others immediately sat down, each at 'his' or 'her' own place and immediately started work. Zafir came up to me and said confidingly:

Just a few basic things so that there are no mistakes.

A short course in filling envelopes?

Something like that. So, like this, began Zafir, the shift leader and personal friend of the Great Sikh, former café-owner from Bijeljina, Bosnia and Herzegovina, owner of a large metallic blue van (earned by filling envelopes), and a little mobile phone.

These are size 10 envelopes, 9 ½ by 4 1/8 inches.

What's that in centimetres? I ask.

It doesn't matter, now listen, Zafir raised his voice a little because I had interrupted his train of thought.

First you have to separate the sticky part of the envelope so that you don't waste time when you're filling it. Every one of you gets a thousand. These are your envelopes. You separate the sticky part of the envelope with another envelope by putting it into that sticky part with one swift movement – like this. Try.

To start with I was quite clumsy. Then I told myself: *Tea, get a grip. They can't be better at filling envelopes than you.* Altogether, throughout my stay in that Sikh's cellar filling envelopes I carried on a very lively inner monologue because no one was talking and the Sikh didn't want to put on the radio. More about the radio a bit later. *Then,* Zafir went on, *you'll go to a different table with Esad, where you and he will fill these six thousand envelopes with the leaflet that the other four will fold.*

Weren't there five thousand? I ask.

Don't interrupt. Five thousand – six thousand, it's all the same when you get into the way of it.

All right, I say.

Put the leaflet in so that the folded part is uppermost.

Which part? There are two.

Like this, Zafir showed me. *Make sure that the contents are pushed right in, otherwise the envelope won't stick properly. Then, to be sure, knock the envelope two or three times on the table so that the contents fall right down. Like this.*

Later (after a couple of hours, when I'd got into my stride), I knocked an envelope – so that its content went right to the bottom, but Zafir kept coming up to me warning me that this wasn't enough, that I had to knock them at least three times. That disturbed me, because I had already adopted my own rhythm in the filling process. Knocking them three times on the table would mean I wasted time, and the Great Sikh measured both time and outcome carefully: we had each been given a black plastic tub (like a laundry basket), in which, before we put the completed produce into it, we placed a green note with our name and the part of the work we were carrying out in the chain – filling, sticking on self-adhesive labels with the addresses already printed or sticking on stamps. Given that the envelopes were closed, that is stuck down, by a machine, and that machine was electronic and had various illuminated red numbers that flickered cheerfully in the half-dark of the cellar, the Sikh knew exactly whose envelopes were badly filled and on whose envelopes the labels or stamps were wrongly placed and, which was the most important thing, who had processed how many envelopes. In the end, and that end would turn out to be endless, when it came to paying the wages, the Sikh took all that, all the elements in the chain, into account and consideration.

After about five hours of filling the envelopes, around midnight, I began to feel dizzy. For five hours I had been looking only down, at those envelopes on the table, and my neck vertebrae were not in the best condition. Pain ran down towards my right shoulder, down my spine, and down my right leg, while one branch of pain stopped in the index finger of my right hand, which was bleeding under the nail. That was a small wound made by the sharp edges of the envelope, which I had to lift with that index finger for each filling. Later I caught sight on a shelf of some little rubber caps that looked like thimbles, which, I presumed, you put onto your forefinger precisely for that purpose – the purpose of preventing that small but unpleasant injury. The Sikh had not given those little caps to Esad and me at the beginning of the evening, I assumed it was because Esad had fat forefingers and the little cap wouldn't have fitted him. But my forefingers are slender and the little cap would probably have slid about. (My mother had used similar little caps with rubber pimples on them for massaging her gums, and I've got several of them. Had I known, had I only known, I sighed to myself.)

After five hours of filling, I asked whether I could phone Sara. The other workers told me (in a half-whisper) not to ask stupid questions, they told me in fact not to ask any questions, that was best for me and for my work, because the Sikhs didn't like people asking questions. If I wanted to know something or if I needed anything, I should ask Zafir. As team leader (who got a commission from the Sikhs for each of us and I later discovered that his commission was taken out of our wages), he would explain again everything I needed to know. And they also told me, one after another, that I must absolutely not ask the Great Sikh because it was precisely for that, as an intermediary between him and members of the Balkan tribes, people not remotely as devoted to God as they the Sikhs were, that he had engaged Zafir.

Everything goes through Zafir, they said. *Everything.*

That became clear to me when during the five-minute pause, I went out to smoke a cigarette in front of the house:

Mind where you drop the ash. Make sure you throw the butt as far away as you can, so that they don't find it, they all collectively, all five of them, warned me in a whisper. And Zafir concluded:

Careful! The Sikhs don't like cigarettes.

I didn't manage to call Sara because Zafir's wife used up the time allowed for telephoning. *Call me, so that I know where you are,* Sara had asked me before I left. How could I tell her where I was? How could I tell her when I'd be back? What could I tell her?

The snow had covered everything so prettily. And it was glittering in the moonlight. Enes gave me his slippers with plastic soles which, those plastic soles, were very slippery when you walked on snow. I smoked on the other side of the road, where there was nothing, just fallow ground, just a large space as smooth and white as Sara's birthday cake.

I was hungry. I was thirsty. In Jerusalem they found a dead Mexican Catholic priest, Father Claudio Mateo Medina. He was thirty-four. The autopsy established that the priest Claudio Mateo Medina had simply overeaten, and his excessive eating and drinking had sent him to his maker. They called my uncle Mateo. My uncle, whom they called Mateo, had also wanted to become a priest, not Mexican, but Croatian, and he wanted to be called Mateo – not Nikša, which was otherwise his name. Then he changed his mind and instead of joining the priesthood he went off to join the Partisans and there he was able to use his favourite, conspiratorial, illegal name – Mateo. He died.

Before entering the house, I bent down and very carefully, as in a crystal ashtray, in the untouched snow by the doorstep – put out my cigarette butt.

They gave us each a can of Coca-Cola. I went back to the table for filling six thousand envelopes with my can in my hand and placed it in the corner. Zafir immediately materialised from somewhere:

That's not a good idea. Move that Coke!

Excuse me, where's the washroom? I asked the Sikh.

The huge fat hairy Sikh who had been standing over our heads the whole evening, supervising us, gauging the speed of our work, who did not say a single word, looked at me now with horror, with real horror in his eyes, and said:

I beg your pardon?!

The washroom. Lavatory. Toilet.

Completely dumbfounded, even scandalised by such a prosaic question in connection with a job into which, in addition to his prayers, he invested his entire creative, potential, The Great Sikh, his hand outstretched and of course threatening with his forefinger, pointed somewhere, as though saying *Go!*

When I came out of the toilet, I said to the Sikh:

I have to call my daughter.

Zafir cringed:

You're asking a lot, he said.

Esad also cringed, but he's my friend, so he just whispered:

Don't be a pest.

I went back to work, feeling that I had let Sara down.

It was two o'clock in the morning when we had filled and addressed six thousand envelopes. We had still to stick on six thousand stamps. The Sikh had appointed Mirsada as the leader of the stamp-sticking project, because in moments of immigrant solitude she had invented a swift and effective method of chain sticking stamps on six thousand envelopes. The Great Sikh granted her a place behind the curtain where his wife was sitting waiting, his wife was just waiting for the working night to be over and looked fresh the whole time.

Couldn't we have a bit of music? I asked at half-past three, hoping that this would help drive out the thoughts that were thumping in heavy, leaden lumps into the depths of my skull in crazy succession and at huge speed. I felt an unpleasant, almost painfully rhythmic drumming in my temples. For a long time, there was a rumour that Hitler was a vegetarian, because he was sometimes overcome by an insatiable desire for vegetarian dishes. Nowadays it is known for sure that he had these attacks of vegetarianism in order to reduce his sweating (because Hitler sweated a lot) and flatulence (because he often farted and had some complex psycho-physical problems with gas). A certain Dione Lucas, chef in a Hamburg restaurant, recalled that Hitler used to order his favourite food from him – stuffed quail and roast pigeon. What did Sikhs eat? Had Sara had supper? Was she frightened alone in the apartment? Maybe she was asleep.

Couldn't we have a bit of music? I repeated. No one answered.

I turned again to the Sikh himself:

Can we turn on the radio?

He looked me straight in the eye without blinking, not stirring, though the radio was within his reach.

Now he would pull out one of his 'ks' that protected him from attack, from the devil, that kharpan, kama, sword, or whatever, which he kept hidden under his robes and he'd run me through and then all of them, Esad, Zafir, Mirsada, Halil and Zafir's wife, would bury me in that waste ground across the road, cover me with snow, but maybe I wouldn't be quite dead and when it was summer, when it thawed, stray dogs would find me and Sara would go utterly completely mad and would have to travel alone to Rijeka with my rotten corpse.

Can we turn on the radio? I repeated. With a barely perceptible movement of his head, while his turban didn't stir, the Sikh gave Zafir a sign for him to press the button. A certain James Christie was asking a local newspaper why there were buttons on the sleeves of men's jackets. The journalist replied that historians were still discussing whether those buttons had first been introduced by Napoleon, Peter the Great or the Prussian King Friedrich Wilhelm I, but everyone agreed that the buttons, of which there were usually three, had been introduced so that soldiers wouldn't wipe their noses and mouths on their sleeve, and for that reason the buttons had first been placed on the upper side of the sleeve. Zafir turned the dial and music filled the cracks in the half-darkness of the cellar with the six thousand white as snow envelopes scattered around.

It wasn't on for even half an hour. The Sikh again motioned to Zafir with his head and Zafir turned it off. Everyone looked at me, and the Sikh said:

You're not working fast enough. You're tired and the music is distracting you. Go take a break and he pointed to the door again as though saying: *Get out!*

I took Esad's plastic slippers again and went out into the snow. By law, chain gang workers have the right to a fifteen-minute rest every two hours, but our work had nothing whatever to do with the law. In ten hours, the Great Sikh had only given us that one five-minute break during which I had not been able to call Sara and one can of Coca-Cola. Fortunately, I love Coca-Cola. I opened my bag and saw Sara's trainer. My heart contracted. I opened my purse to check whether I had a coin for the telephone although I knew that I had two. I always have coins put aside for the telephone and tell Sara to do the same, in this city you never know.

First I walked up and down, then I noticed that I had gone quite far away. Then I noticed that I was walking increasingly fast because Esad's slippers were increasingly slippery. Then I took one of them off and put on Sara's size 38 trainer, although I'm a 41. At six o'clock, having absolutely no idea where I was, I came to a crossroads and here, of course, there was a telephone booth, because in Toronto there are always phone booths and banks at crossroads. There were usually four banks at the corners of crossroads, one on each, different ones of course. There are a lot of different banks here. I dialled 911, that's the number for all kinds of problems, small as well as large, and they come at once: ambulance, police and firemen. I said:

Corner of Countryside and Clarkway, I'm lost and I don't have shoes.

I was sixty kilometres away from home. In the little town of Brampton, in the suburbs of Brampton. That's what the police said.

It was getting light when I opened the door. It was getting light, but I was crying because it was so magical and quiet, it was snowing, but I was crying, while Sara was sitting on a chair, quite upright and almost rigid, with violet rings under her blue eyes. Then I sat down as well and Sara said:

Was it terrible?

Pretty terrible.

Then Sara said:

Don't cry, write a story.

Then I said:

We'll make pancakes.

And Sara said:

Super. And when we've eaten the pancakes, Sara said then, *when we've eaten the pancakes, find yourself a man to protect us.*

OH, DONNA CLARA

You take a printed form from a pile at the entrance. At the entrance stands a guard who watches over those forms, and in order to get one, you have to pay the guard a dollar. Canada is a land of papers, that is a land of thick, rich forests, which are cut down in order to turn them into paper. Canada is also a land of water, so that in addition to paper there is also cheap electricity, only that's not part of this story. But Canada is a land of very thrifty people. Although food, for instance, is thrown away in huge quantities, despite the fact that there are many cookbooks especially devised for recycling everything left over from a meal and provisions (because Canada is among the first countries in the world when it comes to recycling everything), paper is kept (so that it can be recycled). Cookbooks for recycling edible leftovers are so luxuriously produced that they are more expensive than a Dostoevsky, for instance, but among other things that's because Dostoevsky is old and the cookbooks are new. Few people read Dostoevsky here, so its market price is low. The cookbooks are on the whole bought by an elite, although not the ones for preparing meals from leftovers, because the elite doesn't eat leftovers but rather French cuisine. The poor, black, yellow and white, local and immigrant, cannot afford cookbooks like that so, if it happens that those poor people ever have any leftovers on the table, they are thrown away. A lot of food is thrown away here. But paper is kept.

In the former countries of the communist bloc, especially those which had carried out their revolutions towards the end of the twentieth century – not remotely velvetly but very bloodily – and those bloody historical upheavals were exploited by so-called magnates, former warehouse employees, drivers, village teachers, managers of community centres, the people who twist a toothpick between their teeth and carry small black plastic combs in the top pocket of their jacket (and at meetings use those toothpicks not only for picking their teeth but also for cleaning the grease accumulated between the teeth of their combs and removing dirt from under their nails), who have come from the muddy or stony backwaters of the Lika and Herzegovina regions, in the hands of those magnates, there are always problems with paper. Importing paper from Canada is a profitable business, so if a small independent entrepreneur from a small independent country in the former European communist bloc wants to get involved in a small independent affair connected with such importing (of paper), that wish can cost him his life. There are large sums circulating in business connected with importing and exporting paper. That's why the Canadians guard their paper. So that they can export it. That's why various institutions have guards at their entrances making sure that printed forms are economically and sensibly distributed.

So, when Sara's friend Anja moved from Toronto to Ottawa, we set off that same day to get a cat. That had been the agreement I had gone along with. That a cat should be a replacement of Anja for Sara. The cat would be called Tina, that's what Sara decided.

The institution where the guard watches over the printed sheets is called the Toronto Humane Society, and the printed sheets are entitled, in greasy green letters: Profile of Cats and People and each contains three copies of four sheets. The corridors are full of humane people who come to adopt a dog or a cat. Along the corridors are small booths, each with a desk and two or three chairs, where, after a loudspeaker calls out their number (because numbers are given out as in large meat markets, for instance), the potential adopters (of cats and dogs) and members of their family come for a psychological-emotional-material-moral screening, that is for triage. A social worker checks the information on the forms, and it happens that she gets so carried away, giving her imagination free rein, that in addition to weighing up the adopters with a sharp eye (but out of its corner) the whole time, she interrogates them, on top of the information given in the printed forms, she asks a lot, about all kinds of personal matters, so, if they are at all in their right minds, the man (or woman) must wonder what on earth that has to do with the social worker? And they think: do they keep all this information acquired through an invisible camera in a large personal file? And all that, this whole official interview, seems as though the man (or woman) was sitting in a police station, as if a law had been infringed and they had been detained. The forms were, otherwise, very detailed. They wanted to know:

- Name and surname
- Telephone number – home, work;
- Do you live in a house or an apartment (on which floor?)
- Are you the owner or a tenant?
- How long have you lived at this address (date and year)
- Identity card number
- Driving licence number
- Passport number
- Numbers of other identification documents

Then they (the forms) ask:

- What made you decide to visit our home for abandoned cats? (Please give a detailed response: our reputation, advice from a friend, a previously adopted cat, advert in the *Toronto Star*, the *Toronto Sun*, in local newspapers, on cable tv, on the Internet, something else)

Then there are three columns:

column a) history of your pet

column b) you and your household

column c) you and your new pet – hopes and expectations

Filling out the form could take time, but Sara and I skipped some of the headings and in others wrote quite vague answers. So, for instance, to the question 'What reasons led you to adopt a cat?' we replied – personal.

Afterwards that fat, strict woman asked:

What were your personal reasons?

I said: *They're personal.*

My response upset the feline and canine social worker and she snapped:

Co-operate, please.

I thought: *This isn't going to end well,* but Sara whispered:

Tell her anything or they'll screw us.

I dug in my heels and repeated my response, because she was waiting and her expression was very calm, very hard and very cold. I said again:

Personal reasons are not for the public.

Sara whispered again: *She'll think we've got sexual and perverse designs on that cat. They always have sexual and perverse notions on their minds. Say something.*

I said: *We have no sexual or perverse designs on the cat.*

Then she permitted us to look at the cats in order to choose one, and she took four copies of our forms to her boss in a special office with a thick door, where it (the form) was submitted to a detailed analysis.

While we looked at the cats, the green letters of the question-naire flickered in front of my eyes. [45]

---

45 HISTORY OF YOUR PET

– Do you already have a pet? (Yes or no, list them)

– Are these pets vaccinated? (yes …, no …)

– Are they neutered? (yes …, no …)

– How long have you owned these pets?

– Have you owned a cat before? (yes …, no …)

– If you have, what happened to it?

– Did that cat live inside …, outside …, both …? (delete what does not apply)

– Do you have your own vet? (yes …, no … – delete). If you do, give his or her name. If you do not, give the name of a vet you would like to register with.

YOU AND YOUR HOUSEHOLD

– Your age: under 18 …, 18 – 24 …, 25 – 30 …, 30 – 44 …, 45 – 65 …, over 65 … (delete)

– Number of members of the household … … ?

– Do you have children? (yes …, no …)

– Give their ages … … … … … … … … … … … … … … … … ….

– Role, tasks and responsibilities of your children in the care of the pet (cat): feeding …, cleaning the litter tray …, company ….

– Is any member of your household allergic to cats? Yes … , no …, don't know … (delete)

– Length of time you spend outside the house:

At home all day …, out of the house for half the day …, absent between 7 and 10 hours a day … .

– If you travel (holiday, family reasons, emergencies), who will look after the cat? … … … … … … … … … … … … … … … … ….

– Have you adopted a cat from us before? (yes …, no …)

– If you have, what happened to that cat?

… …

YOU AND YOUR PET – HOPES AND EXPECTATIONS

– Give your reasons for adoption: company … , mouse hunting … , breed-ing… , other … … (explain in detail.)

– Are you adopting a cat for yourself … , for a family member …, for someone else ….

The cats in the Toronto Humane Society live in two, perhaps three large rooms filled with cages on several shelves. The cats in the cages sit or doze, because the cages are quite small. There are all kinds of cats, some short-haired, some long-haired, there are grey ones, black ones, ginger or tabby ones. On the whole they are fat and old, but well looked-after. On the front of each cage hangs that cat's identification card. It contains information about the nature of the cat in the cage, whether and when it was vaccinated and/or neutered, the name it was given and where it was found or who brought it in (returned it). These cards (like the printed forms) are also green. When we noticed a very torn card, hanging in shreds and barely attached to the cage, we decided on that cat because we concluded that it must be lively, that it did not accept the fate that had befallen it, that it wanted to get out. Otherwise, these cages reminded one of small prison cells and I recalled that in Pula in 1923, during the time of Fascist Italy, prisoners were brought into court in very similar cages, only big ones, for people, while young

---

– What will you do with the cat if you move?

– Who will be mainly responsible for the welfare of this cat (food, paying for food and vet's services)

– Will you have this cat neutered? (yes ..., no ...)

– Will you remove its claws? (yes ..., no ...)

– Will the cat be allowed to go outside? No, never ..., whenever it likes ..., only at night ..., only during the day ..., sometimes ... (specify in what circumstances)

– How often to you intend to visit a vet with this cat? ... ...

– How much do you estimate that the cat will cost you annually? $200 – $300 ....., $400 – $500 ....., $600 – $700 ....., $800 --$900 ....

– How long do you intend to keep the cat?

– What feline behaviour is unacceptable to you?

At the end of the questionnaire, it says:

By signing, I confirm that all of the above is the truth and should it be found not to be, I accept the possibility that my adoption may be refused.

people carried out a diversion in the power station and the courtroom was left without electricity and the spectators started to light matches (an historically noted sign of civil resistance), so I waited for something like that to happen here, for everything to be plunged into darkness, for Sara and me to force open the cage, steal the cat and quickly flee from this humane society into the light of day, into the street, but that's not possible because there's so much electricity in Canada that there are never power cuts.

Tina is a grey and white striped cat very like Lara, only she doesn't talk as much as Lara. As the social worker had not yet emerged from her boss's office and more than an hour had passed, Sara and I went to look at the dogs.

Wow! I want a dog too! wailed Sara as soon as we stepped into the gigantic puppy house. There were fully grown animals (dogs) here too, not a single small pooch.

Unlike the cats, which were absolutely inaudible, the dogs whined and barked, sometimes energetically, sometimes pleadingly. Then it all came back to me.

In Nazorova street, in an orphans' home, my sister Lena and I were taken into a dormitory, where some thirty children between one and six looked at us numbly in terrible silence. Then, like a well-trained troop, so small, snotty, so alone, all at the same moment they raised their arms to us, wailing:

Mama, take me!

Lena gave out sweets and chocolate, the room stank of skin cream, urine, dirty nappies, the beds were cots, with bars, arranged close beside each other, the room was full of beds, and hope trembled and tensed around us. *Mama, take me.*

The social worker called Sara's and my number over the loudspeaker. We went into the booth, she was already waiting there, it couldn't be said that she was smiling, which was strange because on the whole everyone here smiles at everyone. The conversation that was going to decide the next phase in the grey cat Tina's life could finally begin. It was the third hour of our stay at the Toronto Humane Society.

You've written that you do not wish to neuter the cat, said the stern woman in the lemon-yellow trousers. *Why not?*

It's not natural, said Sara uncertainly and timidly.

You've written that you intend to let the cat out onto the balcony.

Yes, I said.

It could fall, said our interrogator.

Lara never fell. Nor did Ivo, Sara said.

The stern woman in the lemon-yellow trousers and pink short-sleeved T-shirt stood up abruptly and abruptly disappeared through that mysterious door. Sara and I exchanged glances full of trepidation. Then we began to sweat because it was very hot in the Toronto Humane Society.

Lena went through the mill before she got her Nina. However, that was about little fair-haired Nina from the orphanage in Nazorova street and not Tina the Canadian cat. My sister Lena could have had as many children as she liked, but it seemed that she didn't want to. I know that very well, because before every already planned abortion she had consulted our whole family, we were all involved. Once I went to the hospital with her, once our father went to fetch her, once my mother spent the night with her in the ward, once our brother bought her an ice-cream cake. We were a compact family. We knew how to share our troubles (and our joys). We worked at it, that is my father began to work on it when he introduced family meetings on Sundays that were, probably, meant to replace masses and confessions. We would gather round the table and discuss what had happened to whom during the previous week. We were all exposed to the others' criticism, but a certain dose of self-criticism was also expected of each of us individually. These weren't Party meetings, although they did resemble them, particularly the immediately post-war ones. In fact, I no longer know whether those family meetings of ours exuded ecumenicalism or collectivism, whether their basis was the Bible or the Communist Manifesto, whether the halo of Catholicism or the Internationale hovered over them. But it's of no consequence.

My mother was more of an individual type, not so collectively inclined as my father. She carried on small intimate conversations in private with my brother, my sister or me, huddled in a large brown armchair that had followed us around the world since 1945. Her 'platform' was more spiritual, mysterious, and she allowed each of her nearest and dearest onto it one by one so as to devote herself entirely to each. But she died. My mother. And her 'platform' now gapes empty. Now we are ever more like these North Americans here, polite to each other, distant from each other.

My sister Lena in fact wanted to have children only with David, and David was not able to make children because all his sperm were dead. That was established at an examination. Then David died, and my sister Lena was a very stubborn woman. She was, of course, terribly sad that David was no more, but she was also very angry.

She was angry with men, so she decided not to look at them anymore and the possibility of embarking on a love affair was out of the question. She was angry with death, and no one's death could make her cry anymore. She was angry with life, with her life and with my life, with my brother's and my father's lives. The only people she was not angry with were children. She went to Slovenia a little before Yugoslavia broke up and there she created fashion items. She bought a 'Gorenje' washing machine made in Slovenia in Belgrade at the 'Beograd' department store on Terazije street at half-price because at that time, as a gesture of protest that nobody cared about their Yugoslavia anymore, many Serbs boycotted Slovene goods in large numbers so shopkeepers sold them (Slovene goods) at a reduced price. She bought an elegant black raincoat with a warm *perlin* blue lining[46], and the label inside said Mura Design, and she always walked with it open so that passers-by could see that she was wearing a Mura design and not be annoyed. At that time there were a lot of annoyed passers-by, who strolled through the streets of Belgrade, with three fingers raised in the traditional salute. Our father had lived in Croatia for a long time, my brother had his own family, I was bringing up Sara and increasingly rarely making programmes for the radio, while our cremated mother lay in the New Cemetery instead of flowing in the waters of the Adriatic, all around her native Split, as she had asked and as we had failed to do because it wasn't convenient at the time, and I think we were ashamed.

Sara: *Your mum died?*

Me: *Yes*

Sara: *She's not here.*

Me: *No.*

Sara: *She won't be coming anymore?*

Me: *No.*

Sara: *Don't worry, I'll buy you another mum.*

Me: *New mums can't be bought.*

Sara: *OK. Then I'll draw her for you.*

---

46 That was my mother's favourite colour. *Perlin* blue, she would repeat, annoyed that we didn't understand. Before she died, she began to reveal various little secrets to us, some to each of us. Later, still sad that she had decided to die and leave us, we joined those secrets of hers up into a complete story, her life. So we got to know her life when she was no longer with us. Once when she bled a lot and the bedding couldn't be properly washed, I told her: I'll buy washing blue, and she said: that's *perlin* blue, that washing blue of yours, like the sky above Marjan Park in Split. Now I know what kind of blue *perlin* blue is.

So my angry sister Lena went to Slovenia in 1990, and in Slovenia she stopped being angry. Her Nina was already ten and my Sara was eight and we were both without husbands, without grannies or granddads, and without any help from outside we'd got through the worst (so we thought) – tonsil operations, walking in Belgrade parks in all four seasons, twice a day, shortages of nappies – renewing connections with friends abroad, receiving nappies at the airport, power cuts, and therefore also heating cuts, and the two of them small and constantly dirty (Sara: *Mama, I peed pooo*), shortages of oil and sugar and detergent, pneumonia, conversations about nyumnyums and piddles with mums in those big and small Belgrade parks, viral meningitis, children's theatre productions, all watched, several times (Sara: *Actors, come! Actors, put the yights out!*), solitude (Sara: *Mama, are you alone?* Me: *Yes.* Sara: *No, you're not. I'm here.*), pennilessness, drama classes, music lessons, English lessons, take her – mooch round town for 45 minutes like a stray dog, in a circle – bring her back; beetroot, chard, blueberries, calf liver – because of the iron, steak – bribing the butcher, thick soups, thin soups, local eggs with orange yolks, Chernobyl – isolation, fear, every two months new shoes (little children's feet grow quickest), going to the seaside with suitcases full of water, fruit, frozen meat, to save money, with a potty under my arm, with bicycles and cats (me), with birds and fish (Lena), shortage of vitamins – vitamins came from America and the bottle would break on the way, tooth braces, clinics of one sort or another and in all of them endless waiting and Sara constantly asking something.

Sara: *What's the plan for the day? What'll we do now? Let's brush our nails.*

The helicopter's got legs. Why's it got legs? What'll we do now?
Me: *Wait for the doctor.*
Sara: *Sara doesn't want to wait. Why've you put these here?*

Me: *I didn't put them here. They grew. Titties.*

Sara: *What about me? I haven't got any. My titties are little.*

Me: *They'll grow.*

Sara: *When?*

Me: *When you're big.*

Sara: *I want some now. Big ones. Put them on me.*

Sara was forever asking something, and the mothers and fathers and grandmothers and grandfathers around us listened and smiled inanely so you had to take care to respond in a pedagogically correct, pedagogically patient manner; little keys for tightening the tooth braces which kept getting lost, glasses, doctors' check-ups, orthopaedists – ugly high shoes, diaries (allergic to Pentraxil, sleeps well, sleeps badly, high temperature, low temperature, likes puréed squash, likes apples, doesn't like sour things, can take cherries, not oranges, will eat spinach, dumplings, dresses herself, ties her shoelaces, right-handed – left-handed, draws circles, distinguishes colours, doesn't distinguish colours, has grown 2 centimetres, gained 300 grams, doesn't like the story 'Hansel and Gretel', does like 'The Ugly Duckling': *when I grow up I'll be a white swan,* hard stool, soft stool, throat swab sterile, new words: *I can't gedown!'* There were also arms opened wide for a hug, singing (Sara: *When you're somewhere alone, in the big white world… !*), laughter, a lot of laughter, released in torrents, children's drawings framed, and, in an onrush of inspiration – walls painted on directly,

Sara: *Look, the horse has a tail!*

Me: *So it has.*

Sara: *Sara hasn't.*

Me: *No, she hasn't.*

Sara: *Mama'll puy one.*

old stories, invented stories, short (and long) wise conversations,

Me: *You're going to have a cousin, Nina.*

Nina: *I don't like cousins.*

Me: *I'll need your help.*

Nina: *I don't like helping with cousins.*

Me: *I won't be able to manage on my own.*

Nina: *I don't like people who can't manage on their own. Find a husband.*

Me: *You'll be able to play with her.*

Nina: *I don't like playing with her. I'm still little and now I'll be even littler, even littler than that cousin who is very little when she comes and who, besides, doesn't know how to talk. Do babies have a tongue?* Kisses so soft they make the heart flutter, and those initially gentle flutterings make the heart choke, a small hand in yours (and a question – Sara: *Why do we have fingers?*) Sara's laughter, Nina's laughter, the warmth of a child's body (Sara: *You are my little mama, you're not other children's mama*), irreplaceable, priceless.

At a party here, in Toronto, I learned from a woman from Sarajevo that Canada buys women's eggs. Every healthy, fertile ovum – two thousand dollars. Canada has a problem with natality. That is, not with natality as a whole, because some of their minorities have abundant children, but, I concluded, with the natality of white, Anglo-Saxon women. As the balance between the number of white Anglo-Saxon babies and those from minorities, yellow, brown or slant-eyed, has been upset, there is a danger that in the not-too-distant future these others could predominate.

If that should happen, who would run the banks, who would hold the capital, who would live in the palaces on the estates round the big cities? Blacks? Chinese? Out of the question.

I was all the more surprised by an advertisement in *The Newspaper* of 15th January 1997: *We are looking for an egg donor. My husband and I have everything that one could imagine wanting, apart from the possibility of having children. We are looking for a person aged*

between 20 and 28 to open that door for us. If you are a white woman
(after all!) of Italian, Latin-American, Portuguese or Spanish origin (?!),
physically and mentally stable, please get in touch. A photograph and
basic information desirable. Discretion guaranteed.

Since the advertisement was printed under the heading *Various*,
below it there was another advertisement, with the following
content:

Barbeque, air-conditioner, garden furniture set for sale. Get ready
for summer! Michael 573-8966.

Selling your own eggs, could, I conclude, enable you to live
decently here. One ovum every twenty-eight days. For how long?
So much for envelopes, so much for Sikhs. Addio cake-shops, addio
coaching.[47] A technician at the state radio station would no longer try
to persuade me that Mostar is pronounced Mastar and not Mostar.
Fat Grace, who, with a daily allowance of five hundred dollars, plus
a hundred a day for an interpreter, spent two weeks getting to know
Bosnia – Sarajevo, Tuzla, Mostar, Srebrenica, Goražde and Banja
Luka – and now makes little fifteen-minute 'reportages' through
which she enlightens Canadians about the murky history of the
even murkier Balkans, would no longer explain to me for hours the
difference between West and East Mostar, tell me, with a gleam in
her eye, about 'a writer', very well-known there – she thinks that
he is called Ayvo (Ivo) – who wrote about a bridge over the river
Drayna (Drina, pronounced Dreena) and who was both a Croat and
a Serb at the same time. I wouldn't have to look at the dumbfounded
faces of established and less-established Canadians when I tell them
that I don't like their big promised land at all, because in it I can't

47 In the course of every conversation with my father, he asks: Are you giving
    lessons? I hate 'giving lessons'. Giving lessons irritates me and those whom I might
    be coaching, even more. I really dislike that work. If my father knew that, I don't
    believe he'd ever again ask me: Are you giving lessons? I'd rather sell my eggs than
    coach Canadians.

go either to the opera or to concerts, or skiing or to the sea, not even into a restaurant where they use linen napkins, because I don't have any friends here, because we saw virtually all Fassbinder's films twenty years ago, but they haven't because of censorship, and now they tell me that he, Fassbinder, made great films, and they quote Hans Magnus Enzensberger, whom they discovered in 1996, and bring me books by Hanna Arendt and it makes me sick.

How can you not like it, is it better in your country? they ask.

There aren't many sales and food is more expensive, and the country's been robbed, but it is better, I reply.

Aren't they at war in your country? they also ask.

'My country is just a sad, hidebound and backward province of European civilisation, which is in any case on its way out', I'm quoting the words of our great and famous writer, but they, of course, don't know that.

Isn't it unsafe in your country?

In my country people don't wait to be given small coins in change. It's better in my country, nevertheless.

Then I remember the Poles and Czechs on the little wall beside the jetty in the Istrian resort of Rovinj, who used for years to sell little tins of sardines, padlocks, torches, men's socks and synthetic shirts, all for tiny sums, just so that they could spend a day or two longer in their tents in campsites outside town, their hands were white, cared-for, their faces cultured, and their eyes sad. And I think how sickened they must have been by us Yugoslavs. How we must have disgusted them in restaurants in Budapest, Prague and Warsaw when we exchanged a little bag of 'Vegeta' stock cubes and a little packet of chewing gum so as to be able to gorge ourselves on their goulash, listen to their Gypsies softly strumming their violins in our ear and buy (as we still do) their salami, their cheeses, arrogantly, by the case-load.

They don't understand anything here in Canada. How much history there is in one short statement of a Canadian student, for instance, an estranged Serb from Croatia, when he said to me:

If you go back, take a photo of my Glina for me.

All these thoughts had made me so tense that I could hardly wait for the fat assistant to emerge from her boss's office to pick a fight with her. But she was quicker off the mark:

We can't entrust one of our cats to you, she snapped, still standing.

I was speechless. Sara was dumbfounded.

You can't have Nina, you're not married, it can't be a full adoption, they told Lena in the Social Affairs Centres in both Zagreb and Belgrade. Then the assistant took out of a large bag all the then operational laws about family law, republican and district (eight of them) and federal. Then they relented.

But, here, the assistant went on. *Read all this material. I've underlined everything that is essential. You have 48 hours to study it. If you then understand why you should neuter your cat, you'll get one.*

I immediately asked to see the person responsible for adopting cats in Toronto.

We waited two hours for the person responsible for adopting cats in Toronto to appear.

There's a new craze in Australia. Killing domestic cats. Gangs of thugs, armed with pistols and golf clubs, go on the rampage. In addition, they pour petrol over the cats and burn them alive. In Australia there are more than eighteen million cats, one for every inhabitant. Those cats threaten the lives of various useful rodents and rare birds. They sometimes even eat little koalas.

A certain Richard Evans launched a campaign in 1996. His aim was the 'total elimination of cats in Australia.' He intended to realise that aim by 2020, with the help of a State/National programme of sterilization. But many Australians are impatient. They don't want to wait for 2020. So they take things into their own hands.

John Walmsley, a member of the State/National programme for sterilising cats, wears a dead cat on his head instead of a hat. He says: *Cats are like smokers. They have to be liquidated, completely eliminated. The only good cat is a dead cat.* (My friend from Sarajevo of a different religion suggests: *They could use Zyklon B.*)

John Walmsley killed his first cat – the neighbour's – when he was ten years old.

The societies for the protection of animals in Australia were powerless.

As for Hungary, in Budapest lives Árpád Nick, a world champion wrestler. While John Walmsley was eradicating cats in Australia, Árpád Nick was moving aircraft with his teeth. He dragged a seventeen-ton aircraft eleven metres along a runway. Before each exploit, he warms up for at least an hour. He is soon planning to drag a catamaran weighing 234 tons along a canal also with his teeth. I decided urgently to contact Mr Árpád Nick from Budapest, Hungary, and ask for his help. Some situations are worth resolving only with the teeth (that is, fists).

Sara was crying and babbling:

I'm going to be a vet and an actress. For animals and the soul. For the animals I must be tidy and always have clean hands, for the soul I can be untidy and dress in various brightly-coloured droopy things. As a vet I have to get up early and go to bed early, which isn't at all hard for me, but as an actress it's the other way round, which isn't hard for me either. If we come in 48 hours, that cat won't be here anymore.

Ask if we can reserve that cat.

I asked:

Can we reserve that cat?

The assistant pretended not to hear.

When we were living in Rijeka, members of UNPROFOR would stay in the Admiral Hotel in nearby Opatija when they had a few days leave. The Admiral Hotel has two swimming pools, one inside and one outside. They aren't particularly big. My father once took Sara there to swim. I was very happy.

Once the two of them fed seagulls on Lungomare. Once they went for pizza together. When Sara was little, they twice looked at a globe and 'travelled' round the world. He gave her stamps (a series with flowers and animals); later she brought them to Canada. When he saw her for the first time, he gave her a big doll, bigger than herself and I had to hide it. She watched him shaving, and later copied him. That would be more or less all she saw of him in her fourteen years of life.

The UNPROFOR officers in the Admiral Hotel (Opatija) were lounging around. It was 1993. The foyers of Opatija's Admiral Hotel were pleasantly softly lit. The UNPROFOR officers had copper-brown skins, in part from their postings, in part from the swimming pool. The UNPFROFOR officers resembled one another. They wore dark glasses and body-hugging white cotton short-sleeved T-shirts in the soft light of the Admiral Hotel foyers. There was something written on each T-shirt. Two attracted particular attention. On one it said: I SURVIVED SARAJEVO '92, on the other SAVE THE RHINOCEROSES OF ZIMBABWE. The UNPROFOR officers did not distinguish between the messages. A T-shirt is a T-shirt.

The civilised world is very involved in the struggle to save endangered species. The ministries of the environment of various countries send their people alarming messages about the threat, for instance, to the small yellow-headed songbird of the Sylvidae family. In the wooded marshes of south-west Ontario, Canada, there are fewer than 13 pairs of those birds remaining. In Canada alone there are more than 280 endangered species. Those endangered species include not only two-legged and four-legged creatures, but also various molluscs and plants of course. And fish.

There are only 213 beaked whales left in northern Canada. Seals, tortoises, woodpeckers, bears, owls, swans, moles, are all threatened. The Minister for the Environment of Canada, Mr Sergio Marchi, for example, announced that in the fight to preserve species the priority task must be the protection of the natural habitat of every species. Outside their native surroundings, the animals die. The ministers of the environment of the other developed countries of the world are in complete agreement with Mr Marchi. There are more and more endangered species every day.

The number of hungry children in the countries of the developed West is also growing. Programmes of nutrition in schools are being introduced, because it has been established that in those developed countries every fourth child comes to school hungry so they can't remember what they've been taught because they faint. It has also been established that the number of poor people is growing dramatically. There was great shame in one rich country when it came to light that parents were offering their children for adoption because they could no longer feed them. The ministers for the environment and the ministers for social welfare were confronted by a similar task of preserving the species. The ministers of both ministries were equally baffled and, it could be said, helpless.

The most senior official for adopting cats in Toronto was at most twenty-two years old.

She could have been my daughter.

Listen, I said, *no one needs to underline what I am going to read. I have no intention of coming again. Get that cat ready for me.*

There are rules in this country, she replied. Nothing stirred on her face. Sara continued to sob.

I'll report you in the press, I raised my voice.

That's your right, she said icily.

Cats are more important than children to you, I'll expose you in the radio and television.

Cats are as important to us as children. They are equally important to us. She emphasised that 'equally'.

I took out my radio-television pass from the Canadian national station. The responsible person barely reacted:

Explain to me again why you have written that you do not wish to sterilise this cat.

She'll get fat and sluggish.

Not necessarily. I've got four cats and they are all very lively.

All right, I said, *then we'll have her neutered.*

All right, she said. *I'll bring the cat to you.*

Then we both smiled at each other and Sara stopped crying at once. That's how Tina came to our home.

The arrival of little fair-haired Nina in the home of my sister Lena had also not gone smoothly. Lena was grilled by psychologists and psychiatrists in Belgrade and psychologists and psychiatrists in Zagreb. Lena travelled up and down with two different family law books under her arm, discreetly made-up and with tidy hair. In the end she turned to famous university professors from the law faculties in Zagreb and Belgrade who told her what she had to do. They told her how to reconcile the two different family laws, Croatian and Serbian.

Tina the cat settled in within a week. At first, she sneezed a lot, then she stopped. Her left eye closed up and wept, so I treated it with 'chloramphenicol' cream of one percent. Instead of ingratiating herself and letting us cuddle her, she bit us.

Nina also bit. Lena would hold her on her lap and Nina would bite her hand or cheek. Lena took no notice. To start with, Nina hardly slept. She woke at every sound with a terrible scream: *Don't dess, nightime! Leep, nightime! Nina won't leep!* Lena held her against her chest and lay down with Nina on her chest. Then Nina would fall asleep.

Let her cry, she'll fall asleep, some people who gave themselves airs advised her.

Hold her to you, said the children's psychiatrist and colleague of my mother's. *Let her hear your heart.*

Tina the cat was very thin when she came to our home, but she quickly recovered. With Nina it had been rather slower.

This child is undernourished, said the paediatrician to Lena. Then he took out pincers and pinched Nina's skin with them. The pincers had millimetres engraved on them. *Look, she's got no fat. Shame on you!*

In the orphanage, Nina had suffered from pernicious anaemia. She had big blue bags under her eyes and could barely walk. Lena made little food bombs, she would mix everything into a mash: liver, carrots, chard, blueberries, beetroot, peaches, and feed that to Nina. Nina recovered. One day she spat out the mash. She said to Lena:

No mick up anymore!

Lena obeyed her.

Tina the cat soon livened up. She tore the curtain on the window and the one over the bath. She sharpened her claws on the furniture and carpets. She leapt at pictures and they fell off the wall. She pushed her claws into power sockets until she got an electric shock. She slept where she chose.

In Nina's discharge notes, it said that she was self-destructive. She would crawl, and then start swaying and hitting her head against a wall. Lena would take her in her arms, settle her on her hip, with one arm round her, and talk to her. I had never heard Lena talk so much. Lena mostly drew. But then she suddenly talked a lot.

She did all her other jobs with that one remaining hand. Lena and Nina became like Siamese twins. That was how Nina stopped being self-destructive and started laughing. Then she began to talk and to sing. Then she began to grow rapidly.

Before that, Nina had been very afraid of trams, because while she was in the orphanage it seems that she was never taken outside its enclosed garden. And she may never even have been out of her room, judging by how pale she was. Then she and Lena would go up to trams when they weren't moving and stroke them. So Nina stopped being afraid of trams. She was never afraid of dogs or cats, which I found surprising, because it was unlikely that there were pets in orphanages. Nina was also very afraid of vacuum cleaners. Lena would shake a little bag of all kinds of rubbish onto the floor or carpet, then she and Nina would watch the machine 'eating it all up'. So Nina stopped being afraid of vacuum cleaners. Nina was also afraid of water, especially when there was a lot of it, in a bath for instance, because in the orphanage it seems that children weren't bathed in a way that was fun, with little ducks and lots of bubbles, but just had their bottoms shoved under a hand-held shower to wash off the shit. One day Lena filled the bath and she and Nina hopped in together (Nina was little, very little) and they slapped the water and splashed each other while I sat on the toilet seat and sang to them, pretending to enjoy it. Later Nina had baths by herself. When she was seven, Nina became the best cyclist in the neighbourhood. She was best at reciting little poems and the best at drawing. She seemed to have 'caught' that ability to draw from Lena. That seemed incredible to me. She swam better than all her little friends.

One day Nina asked:

Was I in your tummy?

Lena said:

No.

Where was I then?

You were everywhere in me, here and here and here, Lena said pointing.

How did I get out? How did I get out! I must have had a way out! Through your nose, like snot? Nina asked, desperate by now.

No, said Lena.

I know I came out of your bum! Nina tried to help.

No, not my bum.

I came out of your mouth! I must have had a way out!

Yes. Out of my mouth, like laughter, said Lena.

Later, when Nina carried on, Lena told her: *An aunty gave birth to you.*

Then Nina confirmed:

I know. When I was in her tummy, I heard her talking to her husband. She said: I've got to go to Australia, now. And he said: I have to go to Trieste. So they separated. That aunty must have died.

Yes, said Lena, because 'that aunty' really had died. *How do you know?*

If she hadn't, she would surely have come to see what a pretty, clever little girl I am, what do you think?

I think you're right, said Lena.

Would you let her come in? Nina wanted to know.

Yes, said Lena. *She could stay the night. Especially if she had come from Australia.*

Don't kid me, said Nina.

Before Sara was born, Nina said to Lena: *Don't die while I'm still small.*

Lena said:

Not the faintest chance.

Then Sara really did arrive, and I didn't have time to keep up with all of that. Then Lena and Nina went to Slovenia, then the Yugoslav

National Army and Serbia attacked Croatia and Bosnia, and Sara and I moved to Rijeka, then to Canada.

Late one night, Nina telephoned us:

Mummy Lena has died.

So we left Canada. To bury my sister Lena. We left Canada with two suitcases (we had come with four) and Tina the cat.

Long ago, when Nina and Sara were little, my sister Lena and I saw the New Year in together. We made a mountain of Russian salad and steak tartare. We drank red wine from our grandmother's fine glasses. Hugging each other, we sang: 'Oh, donna Clara' and laughed till we cried. After that, we would always call each other whenever things were hard. – *Oh, donna Clara.*

Now there are three of us: Nina, Sara and me. And Tina the cat. We get by.

Not the end

CONSISTENT PROFESSION OF REVOLT

While Marko from Goražde, *a mixture of nationalities from former Yugoslavia,* was talking to the journalist from Canadian radio about his past as a poet, literary critic, university lecturer, about his former conviction that he would become ever better in his profession, he was interrupted by passers-by wanting to buy hot-dogs and sausages from him. His story of dispersed or murdered members of his family was intersected by questions directed to his customers – *well done or medium?* Marko seemed to put up with it patiently, but readers are mildly physically irritated because senseless interruptions disturb the natural flow and melody of the words – and what kind of words. That is, on a small (a very, very small) scale the experience of war, and war emigration: an interruption. We feel fury, despair and disquiet that we have been unexpectedly, undeservedly and, in the final analysis, unjustly prevented from living where we had lived until then. Something from outside has interfered with our plans; people and places disappear; we are required to give up both small and significant pleasures, whose importance to us we seem not to have realised; we fear for our very existence. These are the *canzone di Guerra* that Daša Drndić sings. Anticipating the developed treatment of her later major works, such as *Trieste* or *Belladonna,* she combines document and fiction, past and present, the (auto)biographical and the general so as to portray the experience of a war that is still going on, here or there, yesterday or today or tomorrow. As a certain Vesna, an emigrée, puts it: *here we sleep in peace, there is no shelling, but we are waging a different war. A war in our soul, a war in our head.* That war is waged by the protagonist of this novel, Tea Radan – although we nevertheless hear *Daša Drndić* – in the Canadian Robarts Library, where she reads everything that she can find in this remote country on the subject of the NDH (Independent State of Croatia) and traces the way linguistic or even biological purisms rejected in the spirit of brotherhood and unity were reactivated. She wages it when she embarks on a relationship with a man whose mother, as an employee of the Ustasha police, (may have) denounced her own, while wondering whether she would have done that in order to survive or because her maiden name was Weiss. (The descendants of Nazi and other criminals, their sense of guilt or complete denial in the style of Gudrun Himmler, would become one of Daša's great themes.) She wages it between Belgrade, Rijeka and Toronto, asking everywhere, as Vesna does, *why have we come? There are no promised lands.*

Daša Drndić passed away at the beginning of June 2018. The last time she launched a book in Belgrade, in the autumn of 2017, she was already moving with difficulty, but she still spoke loudly about *the right rising yet again in Europe and the whole world,* about the conflicts between our little countries which the political elites, essentially chauvinistic, constantly sustain, but which they would surely not *again* overheat. In fact, Daša spoke about what she had been writing and saying already for more than two decades. The novel *Canzone di Guerra* was first published in 1998. We are now living in a society like the Canadian one Daša wrote about: buying is a cult, advertisements are strident, savings minimal; there are banks on every corner, and many different ones; highly educated people work in bookshops and cafés; there are more and more people without a roof over their heads. *What is nowadays sold as democracy is in fact a great restriction.* What was sold as democracy, we on the (post)Yugoslav territory *bought,* and at a high price; Daša's despair, which breaks through her irony, comes from her awareness of this.

But in order to live as an emigré, as the immigrant, Boris says – *you have to simplify your thoughts*. You have to discard the very notion of 'personal achievement', give up the habit (perhaps it's better to say – *the need*?) of going to the opera or out for cake. You must disregard the fact that you're *on social security*. It's better that you don't think much about what is happening back home. This condition of successful emigré existence – *simplifying one's thoughts* – is something that Tea/Daša cannot achieve. She is maddened by unsolved questions and the unstoppable flow of history which keeps repeating itself. She is shocked that Canada turns out to be a xenophobic environment where immigrants (with university degrees) are reminded that they must clean their teeth and used deodorant because *in Canada stench is offensive to the public*, only to be asked for *Canadian behaviour* in their jobs. Tea's, that is Daša's, inability to simplify her thoughts, her character, her experience, comes particularly to expression when it is essential to humiliate oneself in order to acquire something that was previously taken for granted, but now you have to ask for it. Particularly affecting are the episodes of competing for social assistance, adopting a cat, the nocturnal addressing of envelopes at the Sikh's house. Being unable to reconcile oneself to humiliation may sometimes seem like pride inappropriate to the circumstances. Criticising those who have offered sanctuary may seem like arrogance. Nevertheless, Daša's whole opus, and her life, bears witness to an uncompromising position that leaves no space for what is most base, most despicable in a person – the sycophantic, which sometimes drives one to beg the occupier for love (a military, economic or even ideological occupier), and sometimes to close one's eyes in the face of minor or major crimes against humanity because they were perpetrated by our *people*, or our *friends*. Ceaselessly pointing to the human capacity for evil, Daša seemed herself to have been surprised by its vast scale, or at least she was never reconciled to evil: in 2017 in Belgrade, her revolt was just as fresh and sincere, profound and personally experienced, as urgent, as for instance in her novel *Dying in Toronto*, of 1997.

After Daša's death, editions of her works began to sell out. Her work, we could even say, her legacy, is reaching an ever-larger number of people. What can this society that Daša has left, corroded by political correctness, burdened by an almost police-like checking of everyone's *orthodoxy* in their allegiance to a particular *-ism*, what can it *take* from Daša?

She was certainly not in sympathy with the police or political correctness – every line of her work bears witness to that. After Daša, what remains is her admirable writing, which one enjoys even when the subject matter is painful, and, with the years, ever more so. What is also left is the chance that we will learn from her the only orthodoxy that has value regardless of time and place, the *consistent profession of revolt* against every tyranny of any kind, against inhumanity.

Dunja Ilić , Belgrade, 2019
(from the most recent Serbian edition of the book, by Partizanska Knjiga)

ABOUT DAŠA DRNDIĆ'S LANGUAGE

The main language of Yugoslavia, the country in which Daša Drndić was born and lived most of her life, was known as Serbo-Croat, in recognition of the two main historically distinct groups that came together with others to form the country. Drndić lived in both parts of the country, in Serbian Belgrade and Croatian Zagreb and Rijeka. Her language draws on both traditions without distinction, revelling in the richness of each. During the process of the violent break-up of Yugoslavia, however, nationalists in both Serbia and Croatia found accents and vocabulary associated with the 'wrong' group offensive. Drndić would never compromise and so she faced significant problems in both Belgrade and Zagreb. Her work contains many references to this situation.

Guide to pronunciation of letters with diacritic marks:

Č   č   'ch' as in '**ch**ur**ch**'

Ć   ć   a softer 'ch' sound, like 'tj' as in 'cap**t**ure'

Đ   đ   roughly 'dj' as in 'nee**d y**ou'

Š   š   'sh' as in '**sh**y'

Ž   ž   'zh' as in 'plea**s**ure'

The letter 'j' is not pronounced, it serves to soften the preceding consonant or to create a dipthong, as in 'Jugoslavija'. If the 'j' was not present between 'i' and 'a' each vowel would need to be pronounced separately. For instance, the name Marija is pronounced like 'Mariya'.

Celia Hawkesworth

THE TRANSLATOR

CELIA HAWKESWORTH taught Serbian and Croatian Language and Literature for many years at the School of Slavonic and East European Studies, now part of University College, London. She has published numerous articles and several books on Bosnian/Croatian/Montenegrin/Serbian culture and literature, including the studies *Ivo Andrić: Bridge between East and West*, *Voices in the Shadows: Women and Verbal Art in Serbia and Bosnia* and *Zagreb: A Cultural and Literary History*. Among her many translations are two works by Dubravka Ugrešić; *The Museum of Unconditional Surrender*, which was short-listed for the Oxford Weidenfeld Prize for Literary Translation, and *The Culture of Lies*, winner of the Heldt Prize for Translation in 1999. Hawkesworth was again shortlisted for the Oxford Weidenfeld Prize in 2018, for her translation of *Belladonna* by Daša Drndić, which was also a runner-up for the new EBRD fiction in translation prize in 2018. Hawkesworth won the Best Translated Book Award, 2020 for her translation of Daša Drndić's *EEG*, which also won The American Association of Teachers of Slavic and East European Languages Prize for the best literary translation into English, 2020.

THE AUTHOR

DAŠA DRNDIĆ was a distinguished Croatian novelist, playwright and literary critic, author of radio plays and documentaries. She studied English language and literature at the University of Belgrade, and later obtained a Masters degree in Theatre and Communications from Southern Illinois University in the United States, which she attended with the aid of a Fulbright scholarship. Drndić worked as an editor, a professor of English, and as a TV programme editor in Belgrade. She obtained her doctorate at the University of Rijeka in Croatia, where she later taught. She is the author of thirteen novels including *Leica Format*, *Trieste* and *Belladonna* – all published in the UK by MacLehose Press. For the latter two, she was shortlisted for the Independent Foreign Fiction Prize 2013 and the EBRD Literature Prize 2018. Her novella in two parts *Doppelgänger* (Istros/ New Directions USA) was shortlisted for the Republic of Consciousness Prize and her novel *EEG* won the Best Translated Book Award, 2020 and The American Association of Teachers of Slavic and East European Languages Prize for the best literary translation into English, 2020..

Daša Drndić died in Rijeka on 5 June 2018.

First published in 2022 by
Istros Books
London, United Kingdom www.istrosbooks.com

Copyright © Estate of Daša Drndić, 2022

Previously published by Partizanska knjiga, Serbia, 2019

The right of Daša Drndić, to be identified as the author of this work has been
asserted in accordance with the Copyright, Designs and Patents Act, 1988

Translation © Celia Hawkesworth, 2022

Cover design and typesetting: Davor Pukljak, www.frontispis.hr
Cover design based on the photo by Jonathan Sanchez on Unsplash

ISBN: 978-1-912545-92-6

This publication is made possible by the Croatian Ministry of Culture.

Republic
of Croatia
Ministry
of Culture
Republika
Hrvatska
Ministarstvo
kulture

This book has been selected to receive financial assistance from English PEN's "PEN Translates" programme,
supported by Arts Council England. English PEN exists to promote literature and our understanding of it, to
uphold writers' freedoms around the world, to campaign against the persecution and imprisonment of writers
for stating their views, and to promote the friendly co-operation of writers and the free exchange of ideas.
www.englishpen.org

Lightning Source UK Ltd.
Milton Keynes UK
UKHW011301240222
399185UK00002B/138